HOW TO BE
CONFIDENT

HOW TO BE
CONFIDENT
JAMES SMITH

HarperCollins*Publishers*

HarperCollins*Publishers*
1 London Bridge Street
London SE1 9GF

www.harpercollins.co.uk

HarperCollins*Publishers*
1st Floor, Watermarque Building, Ringsend Road
Dublin 4, Ireland

First published by HarperCollins*Publishers* 2022

HB 3 5 7 9 10 8 6 4 2
TBP 3 5 7 9 10 8 6 4

A catalogue record of this book is available from the British Library

HB ISBN 978-0-00-853644-2
TPB ISBN 978-0-00-853645-9

Printed and bound in the UK using 100%
renewable electricity at CPI Group (UK) Ltd

Contents

PART I: WHAT IS CONFIDENCE?

Introduction

If you're reading this, firstly, thank you for choosing to pick this book up or download the audio. I can't be sure where you are. Maybe an airport, maybe a bookstore or even in your kitchen and you've just pulled this book out of a postage envelope. You might still be a bit unsure how a book about confidence could truly impact you and whether you need it at all, and it's completely fine to think that too. You're now probably trying to gauge whether or not this book, my book, goes to the forefront of your attention or whether it takes a place next to the other books you've started before and that you'll 'get around to finishing'. So I'll be as succinct as possible introducing my findings on the subject of confidence, and hopefully you'll feel inspired to keep reading, just as I've felt inspired writing it.

The person who loves walking will walk further than the person who loves the destination. The reason I say this is because confidence isn't simply an end goal, it's a critical part of the journey influencing the direction of your existing path. A small change in direction now can amount to vast differences in the end destination as time goes on. I've accumulated and assimilated a lot of research, ideas and standpoints on the vast topic of confidence and I've come to realise that there are three places within your life that confidence plays the biggest role and has the most impact: Your **career**, your **relationships** and **how enjoyable your life is**. All I'm asking from you at this early stage is to consider the implications not of *gaining* confidence to begin with, but of *lacking* confidence within these elernents of your life for the foreseeable future. How does that make you feel?

There are so many things in this book that I didn't know before researching and writing it; I've been on a journey of discovery and I think I can profoundly impact and benefit whoever gives me the time of day to listen to or to read what I've learned and realised during my time writing this book, and before it.

It's time for you to decide whether you turn this page to the next and embark on this journey or if you leave me on the shelf, whether at home or in the bookstore. I think personally it's a bit of a shame that so many people live lives without exploring their true potential, that people live lives shying away from opportunities and are living each day fearing things that should not be feared.

You're 250 pages away from discovering who you really are, what you can really accomplish and what you should be doing from here on in. I'm not just excited for you to read this book, I'm confident you'll become a better version of yourself because of it.

So let's begin, shall we?
James

Confidence (noun)

I've been writing books for several years now, and so many times I have taken a word and simply presented its meaning beneath it. However, with confidence there is actually so much nuance for such a commonly used word, the reason I can't simply give you its meaning is because this single word has so many different meanings. I'm going to attempt to not only give you some clarity surrounding confidence, but also to help you understand truly what it is, why we need it and how it can change our lives. If I was to ask you for a moment 'what do you associate confidence with?' would it be happiness or sadness? An open mindset or a fixed mindset? Would it be a motivated person or someone not making the most of their time alive? Would a confident person be worried or would they be excited? Would they be afraid or would they be brave? Would someone described by their friends as confident live their life with the glass half empty or would they see their surroundings as full? Before we embark much further into all these questions, let's initially break down some of the forms of confidence we run into with people we meet, know and surround ourselves with.

Epistemic confidence

Epistemic means 'related to knowledge'. A very simple way of understanding this form of confidence is to tie it to an amount of certainty you have in a situation. For instance, you may say to your mates, 'There's a 99 per cent chance I'll be free that weekend.' You may say something else along the lines of, 'I guarantee if we take this route, it will be quicker.' However, this type of confidence isn't always clear, or rational. On one end of the spectrum of epistemic confidence we can look at drivers who are overconfident with their competency at driving. This is based on their knowledge of how good they think they are. Yet almost contradictingly the same people who think they're good drivers experience a sense of imposter syndrome whenever they are promoted at work or put in a position of responsibility. So, if this type of confidence relates to the certainty of one's own competence then can it be trusted? In some situations where you know more than anyone else in the room about a certain topic, then perhaps, but in many cases this type of confidence (or a lack of it) has not been tested and, in my opinion, should be questioned.

Social confidence

This is typically how you would act in a group setting, usually out and about. This is how you hold yourself when meeting people for the first time, how you act, how you speak, what you choose to say. Social confidence needs some level of courage, and can involve an element of pretence (which isn't always a bad thing). A lot of people may have to work up the courage to be in a social setting and to present themselves, express how they are, and there is often a constant fear for a lot of people that they will say or do something wrong. This isn't just in group social settings: you can also experience this in a more public domain, such as a commercial gym for instance. The fear stems from being worried you're doing something wrong or that you don't belong in that environment. Human beings fear negative attention, we see this on social media too. I expect the majority of people would rather say nothing than be potentially criticised for what they do say.

Self-confidence

'I don't think it's bragging to say I'm something special.'

Muhammad Ali

Self-confidence is the knowledge that you're able to face a task in hand, a sureness in your own ability, usually within a specific situation or environment. Confidence is generally seen as a desirable trait, especially in sports where it's held in high regard and even a necessity. To quote Henry Ford, 'Whether you think you can, or you think you can't – you're right.' Whether it's Muhammad Ali preparing for a fight or a person getting ready for an interview or attempting to chat someone up, your mindset as to what you believe the outcome *can be* will play a massive role in what the outcome *will be*. Self-confidence and arrogance can sometimes be seen to be only a hair's width apart. Arrogance, as I'll explain later in the book, is not such a sought-after trait in sports, or in life outside it, so I'll be exploring these differences and how we can harness the positive traits and impacts of self-confidence.

Gut confidence

Some things just feel right. Often, we're told we just need to trust our 'gut instinct' and to put confidence in that. But is that absolute BS? Well, the gut and its connection to the brain are very important, more important than people would have thought a few decades ago. Studies have shown that probiotics just as effectively mitigated anxiety and depressive symptoms as conventional prescription medication. (See References, p. 263) But although the benefits to gut health are evidently important to mental health as well as physical, is it something to be trusted to make decisions? Something like this can all too easily be influenced by mindset biases, which we'll come onto later in the book. Where you make a correct decision based on your 'gut feeling' you'd remember it and credit your gut, but other times when the outcome is negative, you may disregard it as bad luck rather than discrediting your gut's ability to predict a certain outcome.

It's about rationalising your feelings about decisions and experiences to make you more clear-sighted about which way to go when making decisions or adopting a new mindset. I don't advise 'just going with your gut', I think instead it's imperative to draw upon past experiences, outcomes and a deeper thought into the real implications of it going right or wrong, and being equally prepared for both.

The reason I've pulled out some of the broadly understood types of confidence so early on in the book is because I feel that *everyone* is lacking confidence in some part of their life and it can look different for each person – we can be hugely confident in some scenarios and terrified in others. I could be wrong, you could be someone who is confident in every single aspect of your life, but I don't think that is ever truly the case. If you're reading this right now and you can put your hand up and say, 'I need no help developing areas of my confidence', I'd actually go as far as saying you could be delusional, or as I'd say more candidly, 'full of shit'.

Maybe no one would ever perceive you to not be confident, perhaps, but you and I both know that if we're real with ourselves there's going to be at least one area in your life that you're avoiding or hiding from. I think this has been the case for so many years, but my concern is that it's never been easier to hide from these holes in our persona through technology, screens and changes in human interaction happening now and within what lies ahead of us in the future.

Confidence Curriculum

'The lessons that we need are often in the tasks we're avoiding.'

Lucy Lord

I want you to think about something for me just before we begin this book. I want you to think about 7 different adjectives you'd describe yourself as. If someone you knew was to describe you in 7 words, what would they be? Do me a favour and please do this, I want you to make a note of 7 adjectives you could be described as right now in your life. These change throughout our lives and it's important we do this. For instance, when I was at school, I'm sure my adjectives would have been 'distracted', 'disruptive', 'uninterested'. But now they would be 'consistent', 'audacious', 'ambitious' etc. So, grab your phone, write the 7 adjectives then set an alarm on your phone for this exact date one year from now. Set the title of the alarm as 'My 7 Adjectives'. When that alarm goes off in a year's time, I want you to write down the adjectives you feel represent you, then reflect on the difference a year can make and the differences the year has made to who you are.

I think if we were to ask most people what confidence is, we would end up with many different answers; confidence is like many things in life, subjective. But I think across the board everyone would say it's a good thing, of benefit and certainly helpful in any if not all situations. If we could bottle up confidence and sell it in a vial, there would be one hell of a market for it. The closest thing we have to bottled confidence is alcohol, but that comes with a myriad of other issues which I'll describe later in the book.

One of the earliest mistakes people make with confidence is thinking it's a by-product of success. People think, 'Oh, it's ok for you to be confident, you've sold books and done this and that.' In many people's eyes they don't feel successful yet, so they think they can't be confident. But really early on in this book, I want you to unattach your beliefs of confidence being linked to success and instead tie it to your relationship with failure. I need you to appreciate that confidence in so many situations isn't reserved only for the successful. It's for those who are able to accept losses and willing to keep learning.

So why do people not tell us this? Why is this not taught at schools? Confidence is a key player in things like innovation. I often think about the fact that it's hard to track or to quantify. There are tests for IQ and you can do exams for science, maths and English literature. You can't test for confidence. I mean, if you were to take a moment to think about how confident you are, or even how much confidence you have, how are you measuring it? Really, if you think about it, it can't be weighed, it cannot be quantified, it cannot be looked at under a microscope, nor proven (or disproven) outside our realm of perception to it.

I have often referred to confidence as being a 'superpower', but I now think to myself that's not the right term. Because superpowers are out of our grasp, they're unobtainable and remain a part of our imagination as we wander off while watching a movie. The danger in labelling confidence as a superpower is this: we can actually obtain more confidence; we can become more confident and we can do it in a relatively short period of time. We are an ever-evolving version of ourselves, we change on a daily basis and become new versions of ourselves over time, like a snake shedding its skin and leaving behind an old part of itself. In my last book, I brought to people's attention the 'end of history illusion' where human beings often tend to think the amount of change possible in their lives has slowed down right up to

9

the present day. Human beings often misinterpret the amount of change possible from today onwards, thinking they're set in a mould and that the future is just a repeat of the present, but an older or more mature version. I remind people that if you truly want to understand the amount you can change in 10 years, you only need to look at the 10 years behind you and to see how far you've come. The morphing of values, persona, ethos, identity, roles and attitude. Sometimes for the better, sometimes for the worse. Life is a project of development, we are the constructors of how our lives look and we are elected by ourselves to decide who we are each day. So confidence isn't a super-power, it's not something that can be measured or broken down when we put it under the microscope; when you think about it, it's more like a belief based on values. Let me explain:

> The only way to truly gauge the potential for change in the 10 years ahead of us is to look at the 10 years behind us and see the amount we've developed to this point in time.

If we refer back to Henry Ford's infamous quote and we dissect it a bit – 'whether you think you can, or you think you can't – you're right' – what we think is ultimately what we believe, right? If we look outside and think it's going to rain, we also believe it's going to rain. Belief, although coined as a religious word, is more about what we think the outcome of something is going to be with some certainty. If you use the word belief, then suddenly you can draw many parallels to how so many factors influence people's beliefs: their culture, their family, their perceptions and their experiences. I pose to you a very important question: 'Can we change people's beliefs?' The answer is 'yes'. So let me ask you one more question: 'Can your belief be changed in what you're capable of doing?' The answer again, whether you like to admit it or not, is also 'yes'.

I don't like to delve into religious debate, this is not the book for it. But confidence is a big part in believing in something that hasn't happened yet, can happen. Elon Musk had belief that rockets could land back on earth after being used to fly into outer space. Yet with his belief in something never done before, it was made to happen. Lucy Lord, a very good friend quoted earlier, once gave me an incredibly influential piece of card with a quote on it. This was during what turned out to be one of my most important years professionally and I'll never forget what it said. I stuck this piece of card to my window and now I travel with it everywhere I go. It was about 3 inches by 3 inches and it had a quote by Nelson Mandela.

'It always seems impossible until it's done.'

Nelson Mandela

Confidence is, essentially, a belief in the unknown, the uncharted territory, the unlived experiences, and only the imagination holds the key to unlocking someone's true potential. We need confidence in our thoughts so we can do the work to make them into our own reality. This book is not a call to arms for faith, but it is a call to arms for belief – in yourself and your capabilities.

Confidence is the power to be yourself and with it brings a slight sense of entitlement, and it makes you feel you're making a positive contribution to whatever situation you're in. If it's dating, it's knowing deep down that you can make that person's life better if they make you a part of it. With a job interview, it's about sitting there really truly confident that you will be an asset worth your weight in gold (or at least a nudge over your current salary). Now, you *could* be wrong, but that doesn't mean you *are* wrong. You may not hit your work targets and the relationship may not work out, but that doesn't mean that you can't be confident putting yourself out there from the outset. You are allowed to be wrong; you're not allowed to think you're inadequate before you even try.

When we can *see* a problem in the modern world, we are usually equipped with the tools to medicate, to put a bandage on a wound, to take antibiotics for an infection, to wear a mask and wash our hands more during a pandemic. But with the downward spiral of self-esteem, with the decaying nature of human interactions, what tools and perceptions do we have at hand to treat the issue? To be honest, I wish I knew right now.

I see confidence as a way to open doors, to be inquisitive, to take more risks but ultimately it is a belief in yourself, to back yourself in whatever it is you need to back yourself in. We're all different, we're all aspiring towards different things and whichever direction we want to go in life we must create the first part of the required momentum by backing ourselves to often just take the steps to begin. Once we have created momentum within our ambitions, we need to keep clawing small victories on the way to keep moving in the right direction, they won't come easy and there will be different versions of us we will need to be along the journey of little wins. As I alluded to at the start, it's not so much a question of what would our life be like with more confidence, but about the costs, impacts and impairments to someone's quality of life without confidence.

My biggest fear in life is a life not lived. When people are asked on their death beds what they regretted from life, I am sure it would be things along the lines of, 'I wish I did this', 'I wish I had done that', 'I wish I had said this at the time'. It's an actual fact that people at the end of their lives regret things they didn't do much more than they regretted the mistakes they had made.

So, I want you to trust me, and by the end of this book, to trust yourselves, to take chances, to make mistakes, to invest in your own happiness, and to avoid regret. Let's begin.

PART I

WHAT IS CONFIDENCE?

Chapter 1

The Confidence Decision

'Be who you are and say what you feel, because those who mind don't matter and those who matter don't mind.'

Bernard Baruch, American financier and political adviser

Who we are, how we act, what we value, what we don't. These are decisions, a compilation of tiny decisions we make hundreds and maybe even thousands of times a day that determine who we are. Confidence, to me, plays a role in these decisions. What do we decide to do when those opportunities arise? Do we act? Do we stand still? Do we stand up for something or do we let it slide by? These are decisions whichever way you decide. Never forget that to do nothing, is also a decision. I love the saying that 'no response is a response'. Doing nothing is still doing something. To not tell someone how you feel, to not express your emotions on something to your boss is an action. So when we look at taking action and doing nothing, we must appreciate that technically, both are actions. But this isn't a philosophy book for you to get lost in, we have work to do so we'll continue.

Sometimes we need to make the decision to put ourselves into situations where we make the decision first, the confidence then comes. I think about the film *Yes Man* with Jim Carrey. In the film, Jim Carrey plays 'Carl Allen' who has a negative outlook on life, so his friend convinces him to go to a motivational speaker seminar where he meets 'Terrence' the guru. He is then convinced to answer every question he is presented with the answer 'Yes!'.

That is not the advice I am giving you, far from it. But it's an example of making the decision first and letting the confidence form thereon. So much of who we are is determined by how we act, but how we act can also determine who we are, or better yet, who we become. I've heard the saying from coaches around the world but after a little bit of research it appears a French writer named Joseph Joubert was the first to say, 'to teach is to learn twice'. When I was first asked to teach jiu-jitsu at my local gym, I said yes before I even considered it properly. It would mean thorough examination of the technique before teaching it; the fear and pressure of getting it wrong worked out to be the perfect motivator to ensure I studied before I began teaching. Not always should you say yes, then figure it out. But for many people it's one of the fastest ways to develop your skills in something. Take on the responsibility to make you do the work you may have been avoiding.

Some tasks I imagine are far too daunting to just say 'Yes!'. Let's imagine you are building up the confidence to train in a gym. Rather than saying yes to every question ever presented to you, you could look to just put yourself into the situation bit by bit. Even just the first 4 sets of exercise, once you make the decision to do those you can over time incrementally build up the confidence to do then 8 sets over 2 exercises and so forth. So you don't need to say 'yes' to all of the daunting tasks, but find the courage to just do some of it.

Is Confidence What We Really Desire?

For so many years, I have sat down in consultations for personal training and listened to hundreds of people tell me what they want. However, no one *really* told me what they really wanted at the beginning. What I mean by this is that hundreds of people probably shared the same three or four ambitions. 'Feel better' or 'lose weight' or 'get stronger'. These answers were the path they thought they needed to take to get to what they really wanted. But this mindset is just a guise to that end goal and I always had to probe them about what that actually was – and I'm going to probe you in this section too. Do you truly want to *just* be confident? Or is there an underlying wish and desire that sits behind that aspirational claim?

Pain points

In most cases, when I sat with people in consultations in the gym reception where I worked in the Bracknell trading estate in Berkshire, we'd sit down on sofas opposite each other where I'd probe away to figure out their true desires. Whether it was to fit in the outfit, or that red dress that hadn't fit for three years, to feel more confident about initiating sex with their partner again, or even to not have to pull their shirt down over their stomach flab when they got up from their desk. Come to think about it, I could write a book on that topic alone, I could call it *50 Shades of Consults*. I wish over the coming chapters to give you the tools to become more confident, but being more confident alone may not be the entire solution. I could have made so many of those clients 'stronger' or 'lighter', but that wouldn't have actually got them

19

what they came to me for. It's always important to find the pain point that sits behind any objective. These pain points are important elements of a sales strategy: if you don't know someone's pain point you can't sell them a solution. In *The Wolf of Wall Street*, there is a famous scene where Leonardo DiCaprio hands over a pen to Jon Bernthal's character and says, 'Sell me this pen.' So Bernthal says, 'Write your name down on that napkin.' This creates the pain point that DiCaprio doesn't have a pen in his hand anymore to do so, therefore allowing his colleague to be in a position to sell. It's a famous true story that is used in sales offices worldwide, even ones I've done stints in. This book isn't 'How to be a salesperson' so I'll get to the important point. You must truly know what it is you desire behind wanting to be confident. Is it to go on more dates to find a meaningful relationship? Is it to maximise your potential in a professional sense to support your family? Is it to perform better in sport, so you're not constantly on the bench? Is it to start a passion or a business of your own? Is it to walk away from something you've struggled to walk away from?

I remind people that you must hone-in on whatever this is, because there are days when things aren't as easy as others. You'll need to think of the pain point behind wanting to be more confident to inspire your actions to do the right thing at the right time. For instance, I want you to think about why you bought this book: you bought this book to read (or listen to) for a particular reason, and the reason is more power-ful than the want alone to be 'more confident'. So, when you're about to confront your boss for a pay rise, you don't just think 'I've got this'; you don't just count down from five or adopt a power pose and expect all your problems to disappear as some gurus proclaim. You need to remind yourself of what you really want and remind yourself of the pain it is inflicting every day it goes unanswered. You ask yourself why you're here in the first place and you respond to that question with the answer, 'I feel undervalued at work.' There it is, the pain point. You then use that to build fire in the belly to change it. You tell yourself that you don't just want to be confident, you want to feel valued, that's what you really want. Albert Einstein famously said, 'Insanity is to do the same thing and expect a different result.' So you're left with two directions: take action and do what you're not confident to do, or do nothing. Doing nothing should be the much more fearful outcome. When you ask older generations what they regretted most in life, they will tell you what they didn't do, not their regrets – their inactions are what fill the void of regret in later life.

You muster the pain points to empower you to take action. If it's the harmless act of asking someone if they want to go for a drink, at first doubt, fear and insecurities are rife in your mind. So, you don't just count down '5 ... 4 ... 3 ...' That won't be enough to change your decision-making process! You ask yourself in your mind, 'Why do I want to ask them to go for a drink?' Because you're lonely and you're not dating enough! That is the pain. You can ask yourself again, 'Do I want things to remain this way?' You're left with two paths, inaction and action. Inaction keeps your circumstances the same, only action can change them. What would you rather dwell on later: a mistake or doing nothing? Think about it. Mistakes add strings to the bow, mistakes make you battle-hardened, more experienced and more calm with the next attempt. Inaction and the regret of doing nothing add gravity and mass to the insecurities dwelling in your mind, enlarging them each time. If you're not confident to speak publicly and you require confidence, should you go stand in a toilet cubicle with your arms above your head and hope that your testosterone rises and that you transform into a confident person who dominates the talk? No. All you're doing is airing your armpits, which isn't a bad thing, but it's not really delving into the pain required to create the internal momentum necessary to do things you don't currently want to do. You ask yourself, 'Why do I want to be able to speak publicly?' The answer could be along the lines of, 'My business won't take off unless I can pitch its benefits', or 'I don't want to stay in a role that I hate'. So it's not just about finding confidence, it's about needing to be that version of yourself to ensure the pain point doesn't remain a pain point.

There are many pain points in life we can just leave to other people, such as: injury to a physiotherapist, infection to a doctor, bad back to a chiropractor, or low mood to a psychotherapist. But there are some psychological pain points that require us to solve problems ourselves to overcome. No one is coming to give you more confidence; there is no potion or elixir on the horizon of technological advances. Even if there was, there isn't enough time to waste, the world doesn't need you to be confident; your dreams, ambitions and full potential on the other hand, do. The universe doesn't care if you're single, the universe doesn't give a shit if you choke in your next talk, the universe doesn't give a flying fuck if you never get promoted again or that your business takes off or not.

> 'The universe doesn't conspire against you, but it doesn't go out of its way to line up the pins either. Conditions are never perfect. "Someday" is a disease that will take your dreams to the grave with you.'
>
> Timothy Ferriss, *The 4-Hour Work Week*

It is for this exact reason you cannot leave these tools unattended; you must practise and develop your thinking around certain situations to ensure you're going to do what needs to be done and leave inaction as a choice of the past.

The Confidence Ruleset

I know it's such a cliché thing to say, 'there are no rules', but when it comes to limiting beliefs and the lack of mental restrictions on what we believe, there really are none. There is privilege of course, but this is not the same as excuses, which is what I see on a daily basis. When you go after something in life, do not set boundaries or limits, there are laws that govern the universe, but the human mind does not share the same set of boundaries.

The universe is governed by rules: $E=mc2$, speed=distance/time. I know I'm showing off a bit on my space knowledge, so I'll get back to it: there are no rules as to the boundaries of our confidence. The boundaries are created by us and us alone; we actually struggle to think of anything without boundaries, like the universe. Human beings by nature like to project limitations to all things, especially potential. There have been some incredible feats during humanity to dare to do things others thought impossible and the force they used to do these things was confidence. Adam Neumann, the former CEO of WeWork had no boundaries to his own confidence and rather incredibly built an idea of co-working space to a $47 billion valuated business in 2019 before it crashed to being worth barely anything. (See References, p. 263) What fuelled this rather bizarre yet incredible feat? Confidence.

No one could tarnish or diminish Adam Neumann's vision because he had something in such abundance, confidence. Now I'm not saying you should go follow in his footsteps, I'm just saying there is no ruleset to how confident you are or can be and it is often the unspoken rule 'breakers' who lead innovation and succeed the most. This is also crucially to do with the fact that people as consumers don't just like confidence, they quite literally buy into it.

In doing my research for this book, I delved into other methods written about by authors to help people make decisions when they lack confidence. One that springs to mind is a concept of just counting down from '5' to then take action in something. I remember hearing that 'hesitation is the kiss of death' and although I agree with the sentiment, '5 … 4 … 3 … 2 … 1' and I'm still in the exact same place I started, counting down doesn't add courage to an equation. In my eyes counting doesn't break down or dismantle an issue, it's just a system to try and bypass it. I don't think we can just rely on principles without a better understanding of why it is that we're struggling to possess confidence in situations where we need it.

I'm not a confidence 'expert'; I'm curious, I'm eager to take myself on a journey of learning what it is about this state of consciousness that some humans possess, and others don't. I'm intrigued to know what could change lives and what's a load of rubbish. I want to develop and harness your ability to make decisions better, to enable people to have full appreciation of their abilities and qualities. I am witnessing a decay of social interaction, of self-esteem in people, and I think the amount of confidence that people possess is in decline. I don't want to dwell too much on the COVID-19 pandemic in this book, but it's worth noting that different generations are studied heavily to determine differences in their attitudes and perception of the outside world. I'll explain that in more detail in the next chapter.

Stop for a moment if you're on a train or a bus right now and look up. Everyone is looking down, on their devices. I asked my dad the other day what it was like to ride a train to work before the internet. He said you'd ask someone if they'd finished reading their paper, you'd get into conversations about the news and have a bit of a chat. Over the last 15 to 20 years, we've now got headphones, smartphones, ultra-fast connections to the internet, so why would you interact with a stranger even to be pleasant when you could check what's trending on TikTok? As I write this very book, I am a hypocrite wearing noise-cancelling headphones, but I do often think about how we're decaying the social nature of human interactions and becoming very isolated from each other. AirPods alone as a business generate $20 billion a year; that's more than double Uber or Spotify's revenue. A device that even when not charged can still stop people talking to you.

So we're glued to devices for on average nearly half the day we're awake and we're witnessing a slow breakdown in interactions between humans, then a pandemic happened. COVID-19 changed the world. Suddenly, masks meant you couldn't see over half of people's faces. I don't know about you, but I missed the smile from the waiter or waitress as I ordered breakfast. I missed those awkward smiles as you nod to someone to go through the door before you. Suddenly, we had to isolate, quarantine, distance and limit the amount of people who would even step into an elevator together. Social interactions soon became a fear of spreading a disease. The world of dating went digital almost overnight with lockdowns, clubs and bars shutting to the public. Suddenly, within days your dating identity was shrunk to five pictures in a portrait format and text in a chat box. A quick Google search shows that it's estimated that Tinder, a popular dating app, is worth $40 billion.

Single people have been able to rely on social interactions to meet and mingle with people to find a companion, but much of 2020 and 2021 saw people being confined to their homes for months on end in a bid to slow the spread of coronavirus. This forced a lot of people into the realm of online dating which in essence brings strangers together who find each other attractive. Don't get me wrong, there are plenty of upsides to using dating apps, convenience for one, but the main driving force behind their popularity I believe is to do with the fact you'll get rejected a lot less, or be given a fake number less. However, convenience can negate the fabric in which human beings exist. Look at rising obesity rates across the world, things are more convenient than ever. You literally only need to tap your iPhone maybe five or six times and there is an extra-large pizza at your front door (with a diet coke too, to cancel out the damage, obviously).

I am not saying these advances in technology are all bad by any means, but we need to understand why there is a breakdown and decaying effect happening to areas of our confidence and that as technology progresses, they will only continue to break down for not only ourselves but future generations.

It's never been easier to hide behind a tablet, a screen or even a computer. I mean, if I was to look at the criticisms I get in my line of work, they're quite literally 100 per cent online. That's not an over-inflation of the facts. Never in all my years has someone criticised me and anything I've done, face to face. The 'keyboard warriors' hide behind the barrier of the internet. The pandemic meant a lot more people worked from home, but also job interviews would now be done online. This I think can be a detriment and a benefit. For a start, logistically you wouldn't need to take a morning off work to go for an interview at another employer, worrying about getting spotted as you walk in. Nowadays post-pandemic, you don't even need to put trousers on to get to the final interview for a higher paying job, you could just put a shirt and jacket on and do it over a Zoom call. It doesn't take much longer than a few weeks of skipping the gym for reversibility to set in, becoming physically unable to do what was possible before. Why do we not worry about the potential impacts of the weakening of our mind? Why do we not give the de-training effect of confidence that same weight, pardon the pun. Confidence is perishable … unless we do something about it.

'A man cannot be comfortable without his own approval.'

Mark Twain

As we continue through this book, I want you to remember that your mindset, your outlook and your beliefs are only governed by rules and limitations that you set for yourself.

The Ugly Side of Lacking Confidence

Many of the things that we idolise and aspire to have rather dark opposites, for instance 'financial freedom'. Although this is subjective in nature, the opposite of financial freedom is never a good place to be in life. Being broke or financially unstable can lead to all kinds of deterioration in someone's mental health. Some studies show that being in poverty can double your chances of suffering depression. (See References, p. 263) The same study pointed out that your chances of being obese slightly rises if you're living in poverty, with type II diabetes also following suit. A lack of confidence can certainly be a barrier to important parts of being a human, for instance someone suffering with loneliness could hinder their chances of meeting a suitable life partner if they don't have the confidence to date, ask someone out or even 'put themselves out there'. It's important we distinguish the difference between loneliness and aloneness quickly. The main differences I can think of between being lonely and being alone is the emotional attachment to each state. If you think about it, being alone is still a state of being, while loneliness is more of a feeling you experience as something that is happening to you, more out of your control. Many people, myself included, can be perfectly happy being by themselves, but it's worth noting we can also be lonely even if we're with a group of people.

I remember one of the first times I mixed the two emotions together was when I was travelling around eastern Australia and I was in constant contact with my friends online and on socials, but over a two-week period I remember that I didn't know anyone because I spent a lot of time on Greyhound buses and seeing tourist places on my own. I thought for a second that I was lonely. I did what I usually do and I expressed how I was feeling with a close friend and she snapped me out of it. She said, 'Are you kidding me?' and she went on to explain, very rightly so, that in 5 to 10 years I'd have a family and I'd give one of my kidneys to have some time in the sun to explore and listen to podcasts and audiobooks on my own. It was that change in perspective that allowed me to fully appreciate my situation, some 'me' time. I wasn't lonely, I was alone. There was a massive difference; it wasn't like I had no friends, I just simply was surrounded by people significantly less than usual but as my friend pointed out, it wasn't permanent and all I had to do was talk to strangers to make more friends. So that's exactly what I did. I then used the rest of the time on my own as some self-development time to think and reflect on my life outside of the travelling. I think the pandemic for many people made them feel lonely, when in fact they were more alone than usual, however most of us still had a lot of social contact, just not in person. I didn't like the term 'social distancing', I thought 'physical distancing' would have been more apt. There are periods in your life when you're better off being alone. As I'll explain later in the book on the topic of solo travelling, sometimes building the confidence to do things alone can have life-changing impacts.

Loneliness is a big factor with relationships and the search for love. I'm sure you will have heard people claim that finding love increases your life expectancy and that someone in your family 'died of a broken heart' when their partner passed away. Don't get me wrong, that's tragic, but in a bid to fully understand the implications of a lonely life I researched the topic to find it's not quite so easy to distinguish the effects of life expectancies of people in love versus those who are not. I'm not sure I quite like the fact that the United States Social Securities website has a life expectancy calculator to use to determine how many years you have left to live on average. I'll take 48.3 years, but it didn't ask me marital status or anything beyond gender and age. We can't draw too much from the claims because the fact of the matter is that healthier people are more likely to get married, and I hypothesise wealthier people are too. (See References, p. 263) Think about it, it's the cougars and the silver foxes that are still able to catch a new life partner later in life, not only that but we've seen before that poverty can increase chances of health impacting disease or depression, so that's where I get my hypothesis from. Rather than saying married people live longer, we can say those who are going to live longer are more likely to get married. I also theorise that people who respect themselves through exercise, eating well etc. are more likely to respect a partner because they appreciate the long-term benefits of doing things in the short term that aren't perfect. Whether conceding in an argument despite feeling they're right or dodging the McDonald's, lunch for a salad instead. That long sightedness to make short-sighted decisions based on what you know is right long-term versus what feels right now, will be a big influential factor in love, life expectancy and compatibility.

Confidence

———————

Time

Old people will always try to teach young people one lesson: that life goes fast. I remember a quote that says the tragedy of all of this is that young people won't believe them when old people say it. Then the story goes on generation after generation. Another quote I love that I write in birthday cards is 'growing old is a privilege denied to too many' which was a saying from the famous and much quoted Mark Twain. As we get older, we begin to lose grasp on confidence. Why is this? Well, I think it has to do with the fact we lose things as we get older: the ability to wake up without a hangover, the ability to not wake up sore after a hard training session, we quite simply lose health too, whether bone density or muscle mass. We lose more and more loved ones the older we grow, and we witness more bad things happening. Take a look at a young whippersnapper, for example (a young and inexperienced person considered to be presumptuous or overconfident). Youth and confidence go hand in hand, we dare to take more risks when we're young, and as we get older we're conditioned by nature and nurture to be less confident. Of course, there is an element of experience: I stopped running in the classroom after I tripped over and broke my arm when I was 11. I think there is merit to the notion that confidence does decay as we get older, I feel it with every year and month that passes. I think it's not something to worry about but instead to use as a strange motivator.

I had no problem speaking to strangers when I was a kid; as an adult it becomes a lot harder, but not for any particular reason I could identify. The important lesson here though is to understand this is not a law that constrains us, it's just an observation on our habits as they expand over age and time. Nothing can truly stop you from becoming confident when you're older, but it's important you take time to appreciate how it may have declined, shrunk and withered to the weathering of time. The reason I say this is because time isn't ever on our side, things will slip away from us and no better time is now. There's the Chinese proverb that goes, 'The best time to plant a tree was 20 years ago. The second-best time is now.' I can't stress how important it is that you don't put off the actions within this book for later or around the corner – or to think you've missed your 'chance' or opportunity. As far as I'm aware, there's no upper-age limit to new experiences, learnings and skills. Similar to fitness, confidence is something that takes training, it takes repetition and it requires us to grasp hold of it. It's not an accomplishment like a medal that you win and keep forever. It's something you get and must maintain. Should you neglect it or not respect the work required to do it, it will diminish over time and fade away. They say it takes 10 years to become an overnight success; if people really took that on board they'd probably ensure nothing delayed them getting started.

Financial and professional implications are also big players in the ugly side of low confidence. Where's the pay rise you were promised in your end of quarter meeting last year? Where's the promotion that was dangled like a carrot in front of your late nights in the office? Where's the help you were offered that promised to lighten your workload? The saying goes that 'saying nothing is saying something'. Sure, the promotion is 'only money' but we tie money to our value in an organisation and that ripples through our lives. Feeling undervalued whether in a job role or relationship will have knock-on effects in other areas and it's essential we don't underestimate the weight of not being confident enough to seek what we want and what we've worked for. Lacking the confidence to begin a passion project, a podcast, or making TikToks of your favourite cooking recipes, worried about no one listening or no one watching; inaction is the disease that takes ambitions to the grave, remember. The year is 2022 and the social media landscape is changing forever. For instance, any hobbyist can now showcase their work on TikTok. Even an amateur can add a few minutes to their build time filming their project, editing it together on apps that are free and posting it to TikTok. You can easily add the hashtags #interiordesign #homemadeart or whatever it is and you're guaranteed a few hundred if not thousand views. The new realm of social media is that people are going to be served content not on who they follow but what they are interested in. It blows my mind that every hobbyist isn't showcasing their work on platforms like this. For decades people would have paid fortunes to have their products, designs, ideas and ambitions in front of potential prospects. Nowadays all you need is audacity, that's the only cost required to showcase anything you like. I know a lot of people feel they're a bit late to the party with the current way the world works. A lot of people if you were to ask them about why they haven't started their business, they feel they've left it too late. But I disagree, previously on most social media platforms it took years to build big audiences, that or a stint on *Love Island*. Nowadays it has never been easier to put your passion projects in front of people interested in it. I like to remind people of the beauty you can find in the hard few weeks, months even years. There's a therapeutic sense to creating media for all kinds of different platforms. I like to remind people whether starting a podcast, business or hobbyist account, often you can reap the rewards before the first viewer or listener even tunes in. Too many of you use 'being too late' as an excuse to cover up the fact you're missing the only real thing you need to begin the journey to becoming more confident, to just begin.

A lack of confidence isn't always just in ourselves, it can be in other people. In my early years, I struggled to delegate to other people because I wasn't confident in other people to do the job well enough. Therefore, I was overworked and sleep-deprived and heavily fatigued. It wasn't my own lack of confidence that was having a negative impact on my health and lifestyle but a lack of confidence in other people instead. Now I approach things a lot more pragmatically and appreciate that delegation can not only improve my productivity but also my health. For so many people, it's important to set aside their pride and invest time and build confidence in other people to do things for them, whether a partner, co-parent, a business partner, assistant or an employee.

Should you need to build confidence in someone you don't know, how would you do it? You'd think to yourself, 'Is this person able to do the task?' Then you'd get them to do a small amount of it to see how they fare in the given task, you'd then have some sort of feedback on the task, you'd then probably get them to do a bit more, little by little, until you're getting the person to fully and competently do everything possible within their remit, right?

So, why don't you give yourself the same opportunities to build confidence in yourself as you would with others? If you're able to let a complete stranger earn your confidence in a task then why is it so difficult for you to prove to yourself your competence in abilities to truly build self-confidence?

'We all have our limitations, but when we listen to our critics, we also have theirs.'

Robert Breault

Learning the Role of Autonomy in Confidence

When we grow up we're programmed a bit like computers, with rules to follow, as I introduced a little earlier on. These rules set the parameters of how we live our life; these rules enable us to be a part of society that ultimately we fit into. Fitting in with societal norms is prioritised over ambitious and outlandish character traits. I think most parents would rather their child behave at school than be overly ambitious in a certain subject. Many of us share these norms, these rules and these pre-written codes: green light means go, red light means stop. Don't steal, don't harm another person. On top of that we have other rules in society: get good grades and get a good job, don't drink until you're of age. It's like a blueprint to follow to fit in. Don't drive a car unless you're insured, don't stay up too late, don't run by a swimming pool. Rules, rules, rules, everywhere. Now you can live a perfectly normal life just simply abiding by the rules. Turn up to work when you're asked, abide by the rules of the employer, get paid, go home and repeat until the end of time. Rules and values structure our existence to keep us safe, prevent us getting lonely or isolated and to enable us to contribute to society in general and probably most important of all, pay taxes.

Confidence, like many traits, does not play a part within the 'rules system', it is a state of mind. It is not taught, there is no curriculum in our education systems, there is no real blueprint to follow. To put it simply, it requires an acknowledgement of our own autonomy, and how we harness it while being a part of these societal structures and systems. There are many YouTube videos and blogs on the internet proclaiming to have the simple steps to follow, but when you delve into them you realise they're more about clickbait, they're about hits on the video and driving traffic than they are truly helpful. You are limited by what you can do within the rules of finances, you are limited to what you can do within the laws of where you live, but there's not an open discussion about the fact that there is neither a limit, nor penalty for exceeding or lacking confidence.

I nearly wrote about confidence being a trait unique to human beings, but it's not. Some pets are timid, others very confident. What constitutes their confidence is another question altogether. I strongly believe it is a collation of previous experiences. I mean, if you start off in life and things go pretty well, even as an animal, you have no reason to be scared of much, you have no previous experiences that would conclude to many reasons why you should be. A dog that's had several years of safety probably wouldn't see a road as a tangible threat and that didn't work out well for any of the dogs we had as a family that encountered a busy road. On the other hand, you can sometimes notice how timid other dogs are, especially rescue dogs that have had previous negative experiences of most things having a relative threat element to them, therefore they tend to be more shy and less likely to go near a stranger who wants to pet them.

What I'm getting at here is that previous events in your life are going to be a compilation of where you draw a picture of your reality and this will influence how you determine, see and perceive the outside world and all the elements within it that make up your life.

'Memory is not a description of the objective past. Memory is a tool. Memory is the past's guide to the future. If you remember that something bad happened, and you can figure out why, then you can try to avoid that bad thing happening again. That's the purpose of memory. It's not "to remember the past". It's to stop the same damn thing from happening over and over.'

Jordan B Peterson, *12 Rules for Life: An Antidote to Chaos*

If you then perhaps have a history of bad experiences, you may have a valid reason to not be confident, because your confidence has been influenced by experiences. But that doesn't mean the trend needs to continue, does it? We could then agree that perhaps your current total amount of confidence is based upon all events that have occurred before you, to this day. Perhaps this could be one of the reasons why some people have a higher total amount of confidence than others? Right?

So we can now start to build a strong case that confidence is a state of mind, not a rule, not a law of physics. There are other states of mind, like being offended and the real meaning of aggression which we will get back into in later chapters. Both these states of mind are equally important to note as choices we make with our thinking and behaviour. Thinking before behaviour is a really important understanding to acknowledge too. For instance, if we think about acting with a lack of confidence, it stems from the thinking process that occurs before the action, or inaction in many cases. The behaviour is the result of the thinking. So, when we're looking to impact the result, we don't look at the behaviour, we need to look at the thinking that precedes it. Just before we get into confidence as a decision, let's take a short look into some other factors that could influence our levels of confidence.

1. The Generational Crux

'An individual's age is one of the most common predictors of differences in attitudes and behaviours.' (See References, p. 263) If this was something you hadn't thought about much, I'll start by listing the generations here:

- ▶ The Greatest Generation (born 1901–1927)
- ▶ The Silent Generation (born 1928–1945)
- ▶ Baby Boomers (born 1946–1964)
- ▶ Generation X (born 1965–1980)
- ▶ Millennials (born 1981–1995)
- ▶ Generation Z (born 1996–2010)
- ▶ Generation Alpha (born 2011–2025)

I'm a Millennial, here at your service. The term 'Generation Y' is also widely used for this cohort. It would make complete sense, seeing as the generations before and after are X and Z. Most Millennials such as myself came of age and entered the workforce facing the height of an economic recession. Many of the Millennials' life choices, future earnings and entrance to adulthood have been shaped by this recession that may not affect people of other ages. (See References, p. 263) Why am I telling you this? Because it's worth noting the impact of when you are born is going to influence how you see the world. Some members of the Generation Z cohort have shared their thoughts of what it was like during the COVID-19 pandemic and say that they were treated as a 'sacrificed generation', as was reported in the *Guardian*. 'Our whole generation has just been pushed aside as a problem to deal with later,' a 17-year-old from the north of England said. (See References, p. 263)

Again, you may be wondering why I'm talking about this? Because I think that the generations that came before some of us reading this, and perhaps a generation currently reading this, are living in a time of seeing a very different world to the one that they grew up in – at the height of their confidence – which could give them a substantial lack of confidence in the present moment, compared to others. And this can manifest in several ways, including a disconnect to other genera-tions. I worry that so many traits that make a well-rounded human could be lost to a generation in time. When I say I witness a decline in self-esteem and confidence, it's because life is transforming at a rapid rate where the courage required to be confident is fading and becom-ing almost unnecessary. Technology is not a bad thing at all, but we must take into account its vast impact on who we are, how we see the world and how we live within it.

I'm not sure if we give much thought on a daily basis to what we pass on to our next generations. I'm not assuming that everyone read-ing this will reproduce, each to their own. But we can safely say, the majority of people will. When looking at the vast amount of lineage behind every single one of us, hundreds of thousands of years of generational wisdom passed from one elder to their children and so forth, all it would take is one chain breaker for the wisdom to halt. Something so simple as knowing how to drive a car means you can take on the responsibilities to teach your children when they're of age in an empty car park somewhere safe. So, with this book I think it's a noble effort that all readers see this not only as a journey of discovery and learning into their own confidence, but that of generations to come. We don't know in which direction the world is going so it's hard to predict; as I said earlier, if we could bottle up confidence and sell it as a potion, it'd be one of the highest grossing products in history. So rather than waiting for the creation of that potion, let's learn what we can about confidence so we can arm other generations, friends, fami-lies and peers with the tools they need to reach their true potential irrespective of what they're brought up into, whether recession, pandemic or otherwise.

2. Audacity

Audacity (noun): 'a willingness to take bold risks'.

If I was to put one trait to the forefront of any successes I've experienced in my life, I think audacity would be right up there. Audaciousness can also be held in a negative regard, where the result is shocking or even rude. I think there is a very fine line between these; similar to confidence and cockiness, you'd want to land on the right side of the judgement from someone. Sometimes you'd want to be audacious enough to stand out from the crowd, a bit like 'peacocking' as my friends and I have called it over the years. Peacocking is a behaviour or action done to gain attention and to make yourself more memorable and interesting. It is usually something that's done specifically in order to invite questions and intrigue, rather than being a genuine way of expressing yourself. There is an admiration in boldness, in sticking out, in being like a peacock showing off its feathers to attract attention. Now I'm not saying you need to use this tactic by any means, but it's worth discussing in some detail. In building my social media presence to over a million followers, I had to utilise the tool of audacity. I had to be outspoken, I had to go against the status quo and I'm sure a lot of people would have seen that audaciousness in a negative regard and would have dismissed me as being rude, arrogant or cocky. Audaciousness to me is a tool to be used, it for sure can split a room, but better to have half the room notice you and like you than for the entire room to never know you were even there. What context do I mean by this? Dating? Interviewing? Speaking? I mean, does it matter? Many of the places audacity can be used are correlated; I often see social media as a crowded room of people preoccupied with other things. Should being audacious in some manner get you attention in a room, the same tactics would need to be utilised to be noticed online, right?

> 'Difficult and painful as it is, we must walk on in the days ahead with an audacious faith in the future.'
>
> Martin Luther King, Jr.

3. Effort – why you need to have uncomfortable conversations

I think if you were to survey a million of my social media followers about my attributes or personality traits, I would get a fairly high score for 'confidence'; and I think if I was to point a finger in the direction of why that is, I'd take people back to some of my previous jobs. At an early age, through desperation more than anything, I stumbled my way down the path of having to have uncomfortable conversations, not only as part of my daily job, but having up to 20 of them within each and every working hour of the day. Rewind to 2008 and I'm in a shopping centre in Swindon, England. I'm a sales rep selling on behalf of a company named LoveFilm. In short, they were taking on Blockbuster before Netflix came along. I expect every single reader of this book has experienced a salesperson in a shopping centre, well that was me. I learned many things in my time doing this, such as asking 'open questions' for example. So many people currently doing this job ask 'closed questions' which is a pretty big mistake on their behalf. For instance, they say, 'Can I please have two minutes of your time?' This is easily answered with 'No' or a more polite, 'Sorry, I'm in a rush.' My tactic at the time was to ensure I asked an 'open question' along the lines of 'Excuse me, who do you currently use to rent films?' If they replied saying they used Blockbuster, I could then lead into my elevator one-minute pitch that I had down on lock. You don't want people to be able to answer your questions with yes or no when you're trying to engage in a conversation, especially with strangers.

To give you an insight into the earnings associated with such a glamorous role, I got paid £7 ($13 AUD) a sale. I was lucky if I got 7–10 sales in an 8-hour day.

Fast forward a handful of years and I was facing another uncomfortable conversation with my dad who said to me shortly after I'd finished in education that I should go to the job centre and 'sign on' if I couldn't find a job. I was fresh faced out of university and it's amazing how few jobs there are out there for a 21-year-old when you're not really looking for any and you're spending your days playing video games. So I went to the job centre and as I didn't feel I really needed to 'sign on' I took the first job available, which was a door-to-door sales role for an energy company in the UK. I won't bore you with how exciting a profession it is selling gas and electric to people who already have gas and electric, but after 4 months of knocking on doors all day every day my manager crunched the maths to realise I'd have to knock on 100 doors to make one sale on average. I'd need 4 sales a day, so 400 doors it was.

There is a law of averages for attempts and success. The average number isn't fixed either, if anything it only improves over time. This happens because over time I managed to become comfortable with these uncomfortable conversations and practise the encounters time and time again, using failed attempts to steer the next one in a better way. Back then my averages were 1 in 100; perhaps if I had stayed on I could have got that to 1 in 50. Then and only then can you appreciate how a master of sales becomes a master of sales. Tim Ferriss famously said, 'Success can be measured in the number of uncomfortable conversations you're willing to have. I felt that if I could help students overcome the fear of rejection with cold-calling and cold e-mail, it would serve them forever.' (See References, p. 263) I write this chapter because I want to draw your attention to this part in his book that quite literally changed my life. Ferriss challenged the seniors in the class he was taking to contact high-profile celebrities and CEOs and get their answers to questions they had always wanted to ask. He incentivised them with a 'round the world' free plane ticket too.

His task was for them to contact three seemingly 'impossible to reach' people, whether it was Jennifer Lopez or Bill Clinton, and to 'get at least one to reply to three questions'. Out of the 20 students who took part in his challenge, how many got these impossible-to-reach people on the phone? **None.** The students proclaimed the task was as he named it, impossible. They claimed it was too difficult, they had too much other work on and the competition from the other students was too great, so they didn't really bother. Calling something impossible already breeds the notion it can't be done. That is a dangerous perception of events. How many people are not even trying to do something because they feel it's impossible to be done? The part of this that stuck with me for years since last reading his book, was that if anyone had even sent him a simple paragraph from anyone, they'd be in for the prize of the round the world plane ticket. To reiterate, if anyone had done merely anything, they would have won.

Fast forward to the following year. Tim Ferriss again asked a different set of students to contact an 'impossible to reach' person and told them the story that the year before if someone had submitted just one contact, they'd have won the trip. The results from the following year? Six out of 17 students finished the task and they finished it within 48 hours. (See References, p. 263)

There are several takeaways from this, firstly that should people believe something is possible, it will improve not just their chances, but their effort towards their chances. If we really examine the difference between the classes, you'll note a single true difference: one class tried, the others didn't because they didn't believe it could be done. So they didn't even properly try. So many people are out of the battle before it's even begun, based on their current beliefs.

Full, uncompromised belief in it being able to be done, to me, is half the battle fought already. Your expectations in your success have a profound impact on your success, and that cannot be taken for granted. I always imagine the kid in the dojo punching through a block of wood, they eventually get through the wood, right? So why did they fail before when they possessed the strength to do it? The failed attempts are not a feat of ability but an example of belief, or more so a lack of belief, and how that influences the outcome. I operate one of the world's largest online personal training businesses in the world, I run 12-week challenges every 3 months and I'll never forget one of the first people who smashed the challenge. I flew him all-expenses to Bali for a week-long holiday. I sat next to him at the bar and I said to him over a beer, 'Was it a surprise when you found out you'd won?' He smiled and replied, 'No, I knew I was going to win it from the very first day of the challenge.' This could be the survivorship bias in action (which we will get into a bit later in the book) but I guarantee that the best performers in the challenge didn't hope they'd do well, they expected from the get-go that they'd do well. Expectations are huge when it comes to predicting outcomes.

In David Robson's book *The Expectation Effect*, the author brings this theory to life. Very early in his book he refers to a Harvard study on hotel cleaners. The nature of cleaning hotel rooms can be pretty intense, so the researchers took it upon themselves to change the cleaners' perception of their own fitness. The researchers explained that they were easily hitting their quota for the amount of exercise required for 'good health' simply by doing their job, without any other exercise. One month later, the cleaners' fitness had noticeably improved. They showed a decrease in weight, blood pressure, body fat, waist-to-hip ratio, and body mass index. A simple change in the perception of their lifestyle promoted behavioural change that improved their health markers. (See References, p. 263) This isn't me saying you can skip working out today, it's instead to remind you that our perceptions of our reality influence our behaviours significantly more than most of us give credit to. I'd love to see this effect studied further to really drive home more consistent results, but should the evidence point in this direction it could be a big part in how we approach people dealing with obesity and other issues.

Manifestation/The Placebo Effect

Also known as the 'law of attraction'. This trail of thought is shared by millions of people where simply, you can attract things into your life by believing they will happen, i.e. if you think it, then it will come. Now, although I believe that is largely a load of rubbish, I feel this is a rather more complex subject than most people would think.

> *'Manifesting is making everything you want to feel and experience a reality ... via your thoughts, actions, beliefs, and emotions.' (See References, p. 263)*

Angelina Lombardo, author and life coach

A nice sentiment to think about. But you can't manifest yourself out of a severe illness or out of bankruptcy. I think it is almost dangerous to tell people that they can manifest their way out of situations. But before we completely disregard the impact of our thoughts on our lives, let's look at some certain situations where our thoughts do play a big role in the outcome.

In the 1950s, there were surgeries performed known as 'sham surgeries' where patients were operated on, but only cut open to be stitched back up again, and the recipients of such surgeries reported feeling better. It was even stated that 'sham surgeries' were effective in up to nearly half of the surgeries. (See References, p. 263) Almost half! We're not talking about insignificant statistics, that's huge.

There is without doubt an impact on people being operated on feeling better because they expect to; we've seen this placebo effect also occur with fake medicine and I even had a physio once tell me to put a plaster on a mild ligament strain. I'd twisted my knee in jiu-jitsu and although I was fine, when I got it checked out I asked if there was anything I could do and the physiotherapist told me, 'Well, you can put a plaster on it and I'm sure it will feel better.' I know she was half joking, but her intent was that sometimes when there is nothing to be done, pretending to do something will make you feel better. I can imagine when you give a child a plaster on a scratch, or someone a form of elastic brace on an injury, even those slight compression sleeves, that people will no doubt feel better because they think it will work.

The improvement comes about because of one important factor, the factor associated with the patient's perception of the intervention. It's so important to take note of that, not only the outcome but how we feel about something is hugely influenced by just our perception of what's happening, what is going to happen and what the desired outcome is going to look like. Some old-fashioned ways of healing people are insane, like bloodletting for instance. (Bloodletting was a medical practice of making little cuts on a sick person to have them bleed. It was thought that the sickness was in the blood so doctors 'let out the blood'. Leeches were also used for this purpose and doctors everywhere did it up to the nineteenth century.)

I know what you're thinking, why on earth would people do such crazy things? Quite simply, although now we know these things were not benefiting anyone's health, the people who did these back then did feel better from doing so. Remember, if a placebo works, it still works. Other forms of placebos used in studies include saline injections and sugar pills, and this is a really important part of researching things to see if they really work. Clinical investigators use randomised, double-blind placebo-controlled trials as the best way to validate certain treatments. Non-blinded trials (where people know what they're getting given) may result in a disproportionately large placebo effect. In placebo-controlled trials, the placebo effect observed may be greater for psychological and self-rated measures. Using a placebo in psychological and medical studies is advantageous as it helps minimise the influence of patient expectations on the outcome. From a personal standpoint, I know that although the scientific objectivity to back up the purported benefits of massage and acupuncture are not well known, I know that I feel better after the treatment.

I see a chiropractor in Sydney that I was referred to by a friend. I've always been a sceptic, in fact I would say I still am to this day. However, I was booked to go see this guy by the very same friend. I thought it would be a waste of time. However, low and behold the guy clicked me out and has done for years now whenever my lower back or neck get tight. Whether it's actually doing me good or not, I have to credit him. I go in there feeling tight, I leave feeling fantastic. I'd say even reaching my toes a few days after feels a noticeable amount easier. Whether it's in my mind or not, it still works. If you still don't believe me, look at a child who hurts themselves for instance, all it takes is for the parent to give some care and attention and a lot of the pain goes away almost by magic. If kissing a sore elbow truly worked for elbow pain, I'd be kissing mine after most hard sparring sessions in jiu-jitsu.

So to summarise, I don't think just manifesting your desires into the world is going to do much for you, but what I do think is this: should you expect something to truly happen, it will influence how you feel about things and it will influence how you perceive things. If you put full faith into the outcome of a method, it's more likely to work. I don't think this works in all domains of being human, but it certainly works in many. I think if you're suffering with depression, manifestation is not going to come along and make you feel better. But if you're trying to get your head in the right place for a big work meeting, a super-hard workout or a very important interaction with another human being, and you believe you're going to succeed, you're already halfway there to doing exactly that, succeeding.

We need people to be confident in their nature because advancing forward as people, as nations and as a human race requires confidence in ourselves, our lives and our future. Can you imagine the effect of so many people on the brink of innovation if they woke up tomorrow no longer confident with their ambitions? Like telling the kid at karate it's not likely he will ever be able to punch through that block of wood. If we're going to be successful as a human race, we need confident people to drive forward innovation in areas essential to our survival. This goes from medicine to space travel and beyond.

Chapter 2

Heritability and Habits

What is it? Heritability is a measure of how far or well differences in people's genes account for differences in their traits. Traits can be characteristics that are not influenced by much outside your genes; these are often fairly pre-determined factors such as eye colour, height and the colour of your skin. Now these things can be influenced; if you malnourished someone, they may not reach their pre-determined height, etc. But for the sake of argument, let's look at the classic 'nature versus nurture' debate. Your ethnicity and size could well be determined by 'nature', but who you are going to be in life is going to be determined by 'nurture'. Heritability examines the grey area between the two.

'A central question in biology is whether observed variation in a particular trait is due to environmental or to biological factors, sometimes popularly expressed as the "nature versus nurture" debate. Heritability is a concept that summarizes how much of the variation in a trait is due to variation in genetic factors. Often, this term is used in reference to the resemblance between parents and their offspring.' (See References, p. 263)

I think now we're getting down the path of figuring out whether you can be 'naturally confident'. Similarly, someone may be born with height to their advantage; does the same go for genetically advantageous people with confidence?

The book *Outliers* by Malcolm Gladwell really bolstered my opinion on what I would consider 'natural talent' when it comes to physical ability, sporting ability and also generally success within professional life. It is a human tendency to see success and connect the dots to how we find what best suits our narrative, whether it's 'lucky' or 'privileged' which I don't think should be overlooked by any means. For instance, Malcolm Gladwell in his book makes a point that if Bill Gates was a bit older, or a bit younger, he wouldn't have had the opportunity to spend so much time with computers in the early stages of computing that he did. Therefore, his date of birth was crucial to his success, so there is an element of 'luck' to his success. But when we see people who are fit, healthy and in good shape we should not conclude that they are 'genetically advantaged', although there is every possibility they could be; chances are they leave a trail of breadcrumbs of hard work, dedication, hours at the gym and good self-control around food and alcohol. If we were to look at a large population of men, it would be quite easy to allude to the likeliness that the players over 6 foot 4 would be more likely to play high-level basketball. But the point I like to remind people is that physical traits in isolation cannot limit all potential confidence. Being short hinders your ability to play high-level basketball perhaps, but it doesn't impact your ability to bolster your confidence. Modern-day conversations are far too commonly filled with, 'oh well, it's easy for him' or 'she got so lucky' when the reality is that **success leaves clues**. We should look to the clues before just assuming the reasons or rationales behind someone's success. There was a basketball player called Tyrone Curtis 'Muggsy' Bogues who played in the NBA at only 5 foot 3 inches. (See References, p. 263) So when there is a likeliness that height helps you from a genetic standpoint, yes. There are players in the NBA who are just above 5 foot; there are plenty of athletes who are 6 foot 8 inches who will never play in the NBA.

When we witness greatness in any field, I like to remind people of my favourite quote: 'When you hear hooves, think horses, not zebras.' Although it could be a zebra, chances are it's a horse. Although it could be genetic predisposition to greatness, it is probably more likely that it's an accumulation of hard work. Although it could be luck, it's more likely to be a good work ethic, a good attitude, grit, determination and so forth.

> *'Once a musician has enough ability to get into a top music school, the thing that distinguishes one performer from another is how hard he or she works. That's it. And what's more, the people at the very top don't work just harder or even much harder than everyone else. They work much, much harder.'*
>
> Malcolm Gladwell, *Outliers: The Story of Success*

I think a musician is a good example here, because playing an instrument is a skill, right? There is no way on earth you just become good at playing an instrument, it takes practice, you need to learn your first chord, then develop from there. An experienced musician didn't skip any steps, some learn faster than others, some have the privilege of perhaps paid mentorship which could excel them beyond their peers, but practice and seeking marginal gains would be integral to development when playing music.

So let's for a moment think of confidence in the same way. In *Not A Life Coach* I spoke about confidence being like a fabric that can be stretched, that the mind is malleable to do so if done right. However, right now I want you to think of something daunting in which you may not have the required amounts of confidence to do. For instance, asking for someone's number in a coffee shop. I appreciate some of you may be in loving relationships and this may not be appropriate, but my point can be used in other contexts.

There is a certain amount of courage you have, it's going to be different for every reader. But it's there. Now you may not have enough courage to ask for a number, I appreciate that. But I guarantee you have enough to do a part of the task if we break it down far enough. There is a way we can dismantle the thing you're afraid of, to find a bite-sized chunk we can attack today, right now. For instance, if asking for a number is too much, you can start with saying hello and asking how someone's day is. That's not a mammoth task that requires huge amounts of confidence, is it? If that's too much, just a smile and a hello. It's a start that's required, just something to take a bite out of the much bigger picture. Once you've said hello to 10 people, the next feat may be to ask the next 10 how their day is going. The malleable nature of confidence, I believe, can be broken down into accomplishable segments.

Expectations and Confidence

Expectations have profound psychological powers. For instance, most Monday mornings I have so much work to do I don't get hungry until lunch, maybe even later, as I have so much on. But the day I begin to cut a bit of weight, I'm starving by 9 a.m. My expectations in my mind of being a bit hungrier on a dieting day manifest into actual hunger. When I take painkillers for a headache or a sore joint, within a minute I feel less pain, although I know quite literally the tablet has barely even reached my stomach. It's impossible to have taken effect, but already it feels like it's working. The same goes with sleep supplements, the expectation that they're going to benefit your sleep, the rule goes. If a placebo works, it still works. One of my favourite things to do with friends is to hype up a cheap bottle of wine and tell them it's an expensive gift. How many of us are really part-time wine experts or sommeliers? Personally, I think sommeliers in restaurants have one job, to extract as much money out of you for a bottle of wine as possible to impress whoever you're dining with. To really understand the true powers and potential of expectations, ensure that when you next open a bottle of red with friends you tell them it's an amazing bottle. In fact, 'this was rated best red wine of the year in 2017' and see how many more compliments than normal you get from your friends. 'Wow, well done, this is a great glass of wine.'

Another time expectations are really influential is around pricing. More often than not, people associate more expensive things with being better and people expect cheaper things to be worse quality. Several times a year I run workshops for coaches to learn essential business skills for their businesses to succeed. Part of that workshop I talk about premium pricing and expectations. Say for instance, a phone charger cable. Should you really care about getting the right one irrespective, you'll get the more expensive one because you expect it to work for a long time. Alternatively, if you go for one of the cheaper offerings, should it stop working a few months in, you more often than not expected that to happen for its much lower price.

During the pandemic there had to be testing for the side-effects of the COVID-19 vaccine. Interestingly, people who didn't receive the vaccine and took a placebo still reported side-effects. 'After the first injection, more than 35 per cent of placebo recipients experienced systemic adverse events – symptoms affecting the entire body, such as fever and headaches.' (See References, p. 263) In Britain, £25 million of prescriptions for sleeping pills are handed out each year and some studies have shown that up to 50 per cent of those benefits come from the placebo effect. (See References, p. 263) So interestingly, what we expect to happen can be a causative factor in what is going to happen. We noticed this earlier in the book when we looked at the task that Tim Ferriss set for the students who had to get a famous person on the phone. You don't necessarily need to set someone up to succeed, but you do need to set their expectations up to succeed.

Expectation is an important element of confidence because it plays a huge role in our perception of our surroundings and reality. Expectations are prior beliefs or prior experiences. So much of our previous experiences set up our current expectations. Imagine for instance when I was personal training, I could spot issues a mile off with a client because of the hundreds of people I had trained before that person; a novice trainer wouldn't pick up on certain things because they wouldn't perceive the situation in the same way. I would and have been able to use prior experiences to paint a clearer picture of what is happening.

So why is this so important in a confidence book? Because how we expect things to work out will impact how they do turn out. What's arguably the most powerful trait for an athlete to have? Confidence. I played rugby for 15 years and I can tell you this: when I expected to make a big hit, I made a big hit. But when I knew I was in the wrong position or had my head on the wrong side of the tackle, I honestly knew I'd missed the tackle before I even made contact. When watching people pitch on *Dragons' Den*, you already know who believes their pitch and who doesn't. We are by nature confidence-reading machines. So many people have such pessimistic expectations of their outcome that they're out of the battle before it's even taken place. This isn't to say all expectations are right, I'm sure that you'll still feel pain after a painkiller. I'm sure you'll still have a bad night's sleep when you expect to have a good one, but so many people make their battles uphill by having a prior expectation of failure. Their outcome is biased already towards failure.

I think it's incredibly important to realise that we can perform actions that influence our expectations. Meditation, for a quick example. Should you truly believe it will de-stress you to take five minutes sat comfortably with your eyes closed drawing deep breaths thinking about nothing but the breath, you're going to more than likely de-stress pretty well. Ice baths, although the literature can be very mixed: if you truly believe that having an ice bath is going to help your metabolism, mental health, resting heart rate and recovery, I'm sure it's going to benefit your expectations and for most people that is enough.

I wonder if perhaps people's expectations of ice baths could be influencing the data we're drawing from people that take them. I remember my sister when she was younger taking these drops under the tongue to help her with nerves when she was horseriding. Thinking back at it now, scientifically I am sceptical that whatever concoction she was administering had evidence-based studies backing it. But if a placebo works, it works. If something can change your own expectations, who am I to intervene?

I know all of this can seem unsubstantiated. But I think to myself, blimey, there are hypnotists out there who click their fingers and convince people they're asleep. Maybe giving someone a placebo and telling them it's going to make them feel different isn't such an unordinary feat after all.

The Ugly Side of Expectations

Many subjects in this book are similar to a coin, there are two opposing sides. Expectations as we're learning can have a profound impact on how we feel, and although the affirmations to the hotel cleaners in the earlier chapter yield a positive response, we must look at the polar opposite side of these expectations. In America and New Zealand, I witnessed so many adverts for medication online that try to alter and influence your expectations on your reality. I remember seeing an advert on TV saying, 'Struggling to fall asleep? You've got restless leg syndrome!' Restless leg syndrome is a condition that causes an uncontrollable urge to move the legs, usually because of an uncomfortable sensation. It typically happens in the evening or night-time hours when you're sitting or lying down. (See References, p. 263) I remember thinking to myself, maybe I have that, that explains it, and before you know it each night in bed I'm there thinking about my legs' desire to move. For the record I don't have it, I just sometimes need 30 minutes to fall asleep.

This is why I don't like people putting themselves down or saying things like 'I'm not a confident person'. This language not only infers to their beliefs but it sets in stone their expectations of ability and outcome. This will put someone at a disadvantage without them knowing it. The language you use with yourself is so important, even my friends who are giving up smoking. I tell them not to say, 'I've given up' but instead to say, 'I don't smoke'. Because the first infers that they're trying to stop, the second infers they don't smoke. We saw previously the impact of a placebo vaccine on a healthy person. Imagine the implications of really bad internal conversations with ourselves. So when you look at this in the context of confidence, labelling yourself as not confident, unable to speak publicly or even describing yourself as shy, is going to hinder your ability to break the mould you've set yourself. In British culture, it's almost humble to put yourself down and say you're lucky and not that smart or talented, but keep that as an external dialogue. Deep down you need to remind yourself and your subconscious expectations that you can accomplish things outside your comfort zone, and better yet, you will.

Mind > Muscle

In my personal anecdotes of training, I've come across the sheer power of expectations. Back in 2014, I failed a deadlift attempt in the gym beneath my rugby club. I took a 2-minute break and to be honest I was pretty pissed off. I'd hit this weight the week before with only an 8/10 difficulty according to my notebook I carried with me. I said to myself, 'James, stop being weak and hit this weight.' I remember vividly thinking, 'How on earth am I going to progress my deadlift if I can't hit what I lifted last week?'

After the break, I pull up to the bar and get the lift. It's not easy. I drop the weight and take a little rest sitting on the plates. One of the lads comes over and says, 'Nice! 230 kg, that's impressive.' I say to him, 'No, it's just 210 kg.' He replies, 'No, that's 230 kg' and counts the plates in front of me. At this moment, I realise I've forgotten to add the bar's weight (20 kg) to my total. I'm a bit embarrassed to be honest. However, these emotions subsided very quickly when I realised I just hit a lifetime personal best without even realising. My expectations of what I could lift heavily influenced how strong I was. If I knew that I failed a best attempt, I would have left it there. But because I thought it was something I'd done before, I mustered the strength to do it. You may or may not be surprised to find out that there are coaches out there administering placebos to their athletes and telling the athletes that they're taking performance enhancing drugs. It's not the most ethical practice, but at least you don't have to worry when WADA comes knocking.

I was never a sporty child. I was overweight in school and I quite literally for the first 15 years of my life got picked last to be on sports teams.

From jumpers as goalposts during break all the way to a young teenager. I was never considered sporty until my late teens. This hindered my urge to ever join a sports team, because I'd categorised myself as someone who wasn't very good at sports. Within a decade later, I'd played high-level rugby in New Zealand and now in my early thirties I compete in jiu-jitsu around the world. Your confidence in your ability quite literally defines your ability to get back into shape or to get into shape in the first place. In his book *The Expectation Effect*, David Robson brought to light a study done on people's athletic abilities. Participants took a genetic test to see if they have the 'CREB1' gene which can reduce people's aerobic capacity. The experimenters then at random told participants they either had the gene or didn't. This gave the participants the expectation they were either good or not good at exercise. Yep, you guessed it. Those who were told they had the gene performed worse, those who were told they didn't performed better. The belief in their performance turned out to be more influential than the actual gene.

'The perceived genetic risk changed participants' cardiorespiratory physiology in a manner that mirrored participants' expectations.'

David Robson, *The Expectation Effect*

This is why I'm not totally against supplements or calling them a waste of time as many fitness professionals do. I know whey protein helps with recovery, so when I take it, I feel like I recover better. I know creatine objectively improves performance, so when I take it, I perform better. I know CBD, magnesium and zinc help with sleep. So when I take them, I feel better. For all I know they're placebos sold to me by some cheeky bastard on Amazon, but remember, if a placebo works, it works. This is another reason why we champion the small stuff. Things like 10,000 steps a day is a great target. Resistance training even once a week can help offset osteoporosis, it can decrease muscle wastage and sleep is essential for negating our chances of suffering from dementia and Alzheimer's in older life. Not only is that objectively true, but if we can ensure people truly believe what they're doing is going to benefit them, you can bet your ass it will work for them. Lastly too, I know this isn't my first book, *Not a Diet Book*, but it's important we recap the importance of belief in systems for weight loss. If someone believes intermittent fasting will help them lose weight, suddenly the impact of skipping breakfast is more profound for their goal. If someone believes that eating an omelette first thing will keep them full all day, it may prevent them from eating until later in the day. If someone believes that swishing mouthwash kills hunger, it will do exactly that. So, like I allude to in the book, find what works for you and do that. Because objectivity doesn't equal sustainability.

Neuroplasticity

'Neuroplasticity is the nervous system's ability to change in response to experience.'

Dr Andrew Huberman, neuroscientist

If you look at the definition of 'plasticity' you'll find 'the quality of being easily shaped or moulded'. So, when we talk about neuroplasticity or neural plasticity we're talking about changes we can make in our brain when it comes to learning, memory, reflexes and many more traits. Fun fact for you is that 'neuro' means 'relating to the nervous system' and the word 'plasticity' comes from the Greek word *plastos* which means 'mouldable'. I know it can sound quite complex when we get into the realm of talking about changes to the nervous system, but as far back as over 100 years ago there have been experiments going on to fully understand just exactly how malleable brains are, not just human brains either. Russian physiologist Ivan Pavlov was researching dogs salivating in response to being fed. I'm sure many people reading this will have heard about the expression 'Pavlov's dog' whereby whenever a dog was fed, a bell was rung. Over time, when the bell was rung, the dog would salivate.

'For many years before Pavlov's discovery, contemporary psychologists treated the human brain as a simple box that would process neural reflexes and automatic reaction to stimuli without taking into consideration that these neural reflexes can be personalized by the different experiences lived by each individual and the brain's ability to develop and adapt to new stimuli.' (See References, p. 263)

Pavlov was nominated for a Nobel prize in 1904 and won it. His work is regarded by some as the 'foundation of modern psychology'. There's an element of this plasticity that all of us who have had pets experience: I'm not sure it's 100% plasticity but everyone who's had a pet dog will know about the times of the day the dog knows subconsciously that it's feeding time, they start trotting around the kitchen. This is especially common if there are certain cues the dog has become familiar with, something as simple as just opening a door in the house, suddenly the dog will rush to the kitchen and patiently wait to be fed. I think it's of most importance that we're reminded of our incredible ability to literally change the wiring of how we think and how we act, which in turn tremendously impacts who we are.

As we learn we develop our neuroplasticity, whether it be a new language, a move in martial arts or even your way around the map on a videogame. Not everything sticks straightaway, but over time the connections form for us to know the phrase, perform the kick or find our way to our desired destination. For this to occur, we must be exposed to some form of stimulus with enough repetition for the brain to wire and form connections for you to become competent enough to repeat it and in most cases, learn it. There is the term 'you can't teach an old dog new tricks' but this has been dispelled because neuroplasticity doesn't discriminate on your current age. This is something that is imperative for people to understand, we are not like an engine with a finite amount of output, we are not a weapon with a fixed calibre, we are a canvas with the potential to be masterpieces should we apply ourselves to the right things. Neuroplasticity doesn't just apply to our thoughts, but our actions too. What I mean by that is that what we do physically is also developed through our malleable minds. The first time you step on a skateboard you don't know how the wheels will respond or where your weight should go. But over time with things not going right, you learn where not to step, where not to lean, where not to turn, and over time your mind's plasticity learns the skill. Soon enough, you're in a position to barely think as you skate down the road. Similar to anything else, whether throwing a dart, riding a bike or kicking a football. With that in mind though, don't expect to be 'bending it like Beckham' just because you've spent 20 minutes outside hoofing a football. Mastery in skills takes long amounts of time. I had Roger Gracie on my podcast, considered the greatest Brazilian jiu-jitsu black belt of all time. He reminds me on the podcast that a submission known as an 'armbar' is the same at black belt as it is in white belt (the easiest level), but the same move takes a decade of repeating to really master. The same move, but in your early years it will rarely work, in your older years it will rarely fail.

Similar to exercise, there needs to be the right amount of intensity involved when looking to change the way our mind works. For instance, leg pressing a very light weight isn't usually enough to get noticeably stronger, it has to be the right amount of weight periodised right with the objective of progressing across time. We're constantly seeking optimal responses from our efforts to find the right stimulus, but not too much to be overwhelmed, more isn't always better. There is a unique sweet spot for stimuli between all humans where we learn in different ways and at differing speeds.

'Everything around you that you call life, was made up by people that were no smarter than you.'

Steve Jobs

Plasticity in the young brain is very strong as we learn to map our surroundings using the senses. As we grow older, plasticity decreases to stabilise what we have already learned. (See References, p. 263) In later years there can be breakdown in the brain's ability to maintain such a level of plasticity and Alzheimer's and dementia can occur. 'Alzheimer's disease leads to gradual and irrevocable damage of neural networks, and as a consequence, neuronal plasticity progressively declines.' (See References, p. 263)

The reason I bring up these topics in what is a book about confidence is because many people reading this right now think they're too late for change. If I had a penny for every time I was asked if it was 'too late' to start weight training, I'd be very rich. Yes, it would be easy if you wanted to change who you were as a teenager, sure. But we have the ability to influence our brain's neurons so you can go from things being challenging to things being reflexive. You've done this before too, when riding a bike or learning to drive. If you were like me when you were younger, you went to a very quiet car park with your dad at 17 to finally learn how to drive. I'll never forget getting into what felt like a very strange side of the car and looking down. 'Dad, why are there three pedals?' To find there was a clutch? What on earth is this? Then as you learn to drive a manual you're thinking, 'Ok, clutch, accelerator, lift clutch.' This from the outset is very cognitively consuming, but then the incredible human mind's plasticity changes these pathways for it to become learned. Now for those of you who drive, you get in the car and every single once-difficult task, like parallel parking, reversing into a spot or maneuvering through a multi-storey car park has now become a doddle through none other than neuroplasticity.

You have first-hand experience of your ability to utilise plasticity from a position of 'can't do' to 'can do without thinking'. We need to keep this incredible ability in our mind when setting challenges in the realm of our own journey of confidence building. Studies have set out to prove that older adults would be inferior to young adults when it comes to learning 'new skills', but often they conclude that being a bit older doesn't impair your ability to learn new skills. (See References, p. 263)

So if you're a reader who thinks, 'I'm too old to change', I'm afraid I'm not going to be buying that as a valid excuse, nor is the science.

NEUROPLASTICITY X IDENTITY

If our ability to learn, to pick up new skills and to better them over time is able to change and adapt, then why do we feel that our identity is fixed? If you can become technically proficient at anything at any age, then why do we tend to feel that our identity of who we tell ourselves we are, is set in stone? I'm not saying you just wake up tomorrow saying, 'I'm the most confident person in my town' in the mirror four times before brushing your teeth. That's about as useful as waking up and telling yourself, 'I'm a chess expert.' If we can look through the lens of identity change, similar to our plasticity, it will take time, it will take efforts, it will take failed attempts, but it can be developed. To get better at chess, you'd need to play more games; to make meaningful changes in how you see yourself, you'll need to do the reps.

Gender and Imposter Syndrome

Women are more likely to experience imposter syndrome than men. (See References, p. 263) I've written about this topic in both of my books previous to this one due to its popularity. So many people have experienced the feeling without being able to put a finger on exactly what it was they were experiencing. To recap: imposter syndrome is largely regarded as the constant feelings of being a fraud and doubting your own abilities. I think there are many reasons for this feeling to be more prevalent in women than men. Many industries such as STEM (science, technology, engineering and mathematics) are still male dominated; and the fact that although times are changing there are still many more Chief Executive Officers that are male than female. (The number of female CEOs in Australia back in 2019 only made up 20.6 per cent of the total.) (See References, p. 263)

I don't ever discuss imposter syndrome as a topic whereby I have all the answers. I feel that understanding the emotion is almost halfway to dealing and moving past it. To know we all share similar emotions makes it easier to handle. For years, I dealt with clients who would binge eat food; they felt alone and felt sometimes broken with the idea that they had a screwed-up relationship to food. I told them, 'Everyone does that in one way or another.' Then I showed them 'fitness gurus' posting about 'cheat meals'. That is a binge, it's just dressed up a different way. I'm yet to meet any sane person who doesn't have a day here and there when they say 'fuck it' and demolish two days' worth of calories. Just sit back and accept this is normal, everyone feels this way, rather than feel this emotion on your own. Let's understand many of us will experience this.

'All great men are play actors of their own ideal.'

Friedrich Nietzsche

For the record: Nietzsche died in 1900. If he could only see the advances we've made in society, I am sure he would have requoted himself to say, 'All great women and men are play actors of their own ideal.'

Every single time you experience even the slightest movement in status upward, you will experience the feeling of being an imposter. The truth is that when you start a new job or a new promotion, *you are an imposter.* You're a novice, someone who hasn't had that responsibility before, in many cases. I've experienced this first-hand when I've played rugby at high levels when I was younger. When I turned up to semi-professional rugby clubs, I had to become a semi-professional player as soon as I tied my boots up. Even though I have zero experience in being a semi-professional rugby player, I must take on the role of being one to fit in and to succeed at that level. When I signed my first contract with my publishers HarperCollins UK, I had to take on the role of becoming an author. I've no experience at being an author, but I had to slide into the role and take that upon my shoulders to get the book written. To be a good author, I had to treat myself like an author and work alongside my editor, like an author. Even though I had 9–12 months before I officially had a book behind my name, I had to pretend to be the role, to become the role. I was a legitimate imposter training with the rugby squad before I got picked for my first semi-professional game. I was an imposter walking around the HarperCollins' office before becoming a fully-fledged author with several impressive accolades a year later. I was an imposter the first time I spoke on stage, and I will continue to be an imposter in the roles I have not yet become in life. The first day I am a father to my children, I'll be pretending as hard as I can to do the job of being a dad. All parents jump into parenting without prior experience in the role, so next time you get a job promotion or you're asked into a different line of duty, just know being an imposter is one of many traits all human beings share together. So do it well.

Heritability

I find myself often thinking about where something sits between nature and nurture. In writing this book, I'm trying to find the source of certain traits to understand them better. One word that keeps coming up is 'heritability'. 'Heritability is a measure of how well differences in people's genes account for differences in their traits. Traits can include characteristics such as height, eye colour and intelligence, as well as disorders like schizophrenia and autism spectrum disorder.' (See References, p. 263)

What is very interesting while researching for this book is the studies I've found on how children resemble their parents' cognitive abilities from infancy through to adolescence, which brings me on to a slight plot twist you may find rather interesting.

'Adopted children resemble their adoptive parents slightly in early childhood but not at all in middle childhood or adolescence. In contrast, during childhood and adolescence, adopted children become more like their biological parents, and to the same degree as children and parents in control families.' (See References, p. 263)

This would be a good time to explain to you that I am adopted, which has for years brought about fascination with who I am, my identity and where elements of my personality would sit on the heritability scale. For most readers, you could look at your parents or even your siblings and see traits, genetic and environmental, that you could recognise. I've never had that experience in my life. I've never met a blood relative, so I often sit back and think about why I am like I am. How much is 'genetic', how much is 'environment' or the commonly used dichotomy of 'nature versus nurture'.

It's important we don't believe that nature versus nurture is a strict dichotomy either, because we must take account of epigenetics. The word 'epigenetic' literally means 'in addition to changes in genetic sequence'. (See References, p. 263) Epigenetics is the study of how your behaviours and environment can cause changes that affect the way your genes work. (See References, p. 263) We are not defined by our genes. As we saw earlier, even our expectations can trump our genes. Who we are isn't predetermined by our DNA. Our lifestyle choices have a massive influence on our genetic codes. This causes genetic traits to express themselves either more strongly or less strongly depending on what we do and how we live our lives. Life isn't all to do with genes and DNA code, but many of those genes are influenced by how we live. This is the nuanced middle ground to think about between nature and nurture. It's also been shown that over time as we get older, nurture overtakes nature, especially when looking at things like self-esteem. (See References, p. 263)

Influencing Genes Through Repeated Actions

I think when we see public speakers conduct a talk so well, like a TED talk or a presentation, or see an athlete with a good physique, we think that they were born with the genome to simply find it easy. We think to ourselves that they're 'built differently' to us. It's easier for our brains to draw a heuristic than it is to create a story that perhaps they have epigenetically made the right decisions. That they over time ate what they should have over time, trained hard enough over time. Did their due diligence on the subject they're speaking about. Researched the topics and better yet they build up their ability not through genetics, but with practice over time. I've personally done this myself over the years moving from 'crowds' of 4–5 at my first ever workshop to over 2,000 people at my last speaking event. I often use the adage of 'a frog in hot water' whereby the idea is that if you put a frog in hot water it will jump out, but if you put it in cold water and slowly heat, it will boil to death. I read that this adage has been debunked and the frog gets to a point where it just jumps out. Who has that much time on their hands or the funding to do that? I don't know. But you get the idea, if it was a true adage, you need to just find a temperature you can handle, then heat slowly. (Disclaimer: no frogs were harmed in the writing of this book.)

Think about whether or not you've ever seen a strong person lift a substantial amount of weight; you didn't quite see the years of progress inching up the kg bit by bit until the day you're seeing a tremendous weight lifted. You didn't see the strategies over time of increasing load, decreasing load, resting, pushing and clawing progressions. When you see someone run a world best 100m time, you only witness less than 10 seconds that was produced by 10 years of preparation. Any UFC fans will famously remember Conor McGregor knocking out Jose Aldo in 2015. McGregor earned himself $16 million for 13 seconds of fighting; the world was quick to let you know that meant Mr McGregor earned himself almost $1.3 million for each second of action. Yes, this is partially true but it's also bullshit, isn't it? The countless hours of training, being kicked, punched, submitted, strangled, beaten over years.

Waking up sore, going for a run, eating right, training right, injuries, setbacks, pressure, stress. McGregor, like many athletes, took a decade to become an overnight success. For millions of people, they saw the tip of the iceberg, not the mammoth that rested out of plain sight beneath the water. Conor McGregor has one of the hardest hitting left hands in the game. You can only imagine how many people thought he was genetically predisposed to be a world champion. It's easier to accept that, than it is that he worked tirelessly for years on end without recognition to get there.

Our relationship to failure is a big part in whether we succeed or whether we don't. Only if we accept failure have we been defeated. This was a big lesson I learned recently about the difference between being defeated and losing. I had a discussion with Rickson Gracie, one of the most decorated martial artists of all time, on my podcast. In Brazil the 'R' is pronounced like an 'H'. So just in case you wonder why people call him 'Hick-son', you now know. Similarly, Roger Gracie, the best of all time, should you meet him make sure you call him 'Hoger'. Rickson's incredible stance is that if you give up, you stop trying or that you stop seeking success in something, then you've been defeated. But to lose a fight, to lose an attempt, that is just losing and *that is not the same as being defeated*. When we go into a realm where we can lose, it's not losing we should fear, it's being defeated. Losing usually brings about many lessons which we can learn from.

Fear is something we face every day. Think about the repercussions of crossing the road, the real threat is that if a car hits you you could easily die. What are the repercussions of public speaking? That you may get your words wrong? Why is it that you have so much more fear of public speaking than you do crossing the road? The answer is practice, you've got a lot of reps in crossing roads, so you don't fear it as much. The lesson here? Do your practice reps.

Think about this mindset right now and then what I said earlier in the book about confidence not being tied to success, it's shackled to our perception of losing. Think about Rickson's knowledge bomb here. Losing is not the same as being defeated. Imagine as he locked eyes with his quite frankly terrifying opponents and he was thinking internally, 'You can win this fight, but you can't beat me because I won't give up trying.' I'm not assuming for a second that many of you would find yourselves in this situation anytime soon, but imagine just sprinkling a bit of that mindset to losing. If you can approach any situation happy to lose, with trust in yourself that you won't give up, things wouldn't seem so daunting. Think about someone you know personally that has untouchable confidence. Now think about them in a certain situation that could go wrong. Do they fear losing? Whether a sales pitch, speaking to a stranger or leaving a toxic situation, once you're at peace with the idea of losing, you don't require quite so much confidence to take action. *Losing is not the same as being defeated.* Those 8 words are worth the cost of this book alone.

Chapter 3

Biases

Negativity Bias

'Negativity bias refers to our proclivity to "attend to, learn from, and use negative information far more than positive information." (See References, p. 263)

I often joke around and tell people whenever I feel a short stabbing pain in my side, I think 'that's it, this is my time, I'm done'. For a short moment I think that I am going to die, then the pain goes away and I quickly forget about it. I get a missed call on my phone, I think to myself 'what's happened that's so bad someone needed to call me?' I feel a twinge in my knee, 'oh no, I hope it's not a serious injury', a few weeks later I realise I completely forgot about it.

Our brains always favour negative scenarios over positive; with most topics I talk about in this book the very moment you think about something your mind rushes with negative outcomes. Thinking about talking to a stranger, you think you'll forget how to speak. You think that in an interview you'll get asked questions you can't answer. You think that in sports if you try to make a break away

on the field, that you'll mess up and ruin the entire game for your whole team. You think if you ask for a pay raise, you'll get declined, and you think if you ask someone out, they will say no. This is the negativity bias in action.

You'll have no doubt experienced this in your life, whether the feedback was about how you played in a team sport, or someone's opinion on what you're wearing. You may have had a large majority of people in support of your performance or your outfit, but that one negative comment or opinion will live rent free in your head and there's nothing you can do about it.

So why is bad stronger than good? Is it an evolutionary thing to keep us safe? Could it be that people without this bias perhaps were not so fortunate to reproduce across millennia? I suppose if we were to decide what would be more important to learn from, good outcomes or bad outcomes, you'd want the bad outcomes to favour that decision. Accidently touching a stinging nettle, or licking a frozen pole and getting your tongue stuck, these would be better remembered than a positive experience like a nice sunset or seeing a plant you really liked the look of.

So why is this in discussion within a confidence book? Well, the decision-making process that occurs before you're about to act upon something will be hugely tainted with a bias towards a bad outcome; you're hardwired to think you're going to fail before you even try. I'll repeat, you are hardwired to think you will fail before you even try.

So we're up against this hardwiring issue, but surely we've been up against this for a long time, why is it a problem now? Because now the repercussions are much less severe, but that's a problem too! I'll explain. Too much confidence, too much audacity and a lack of fear 10,000 years ago would probably mean you'd just exit the gene pool earlier than people around you. You'd see the sabre-tooth tiger and think to yourself, 'This looks like dinner, let's have it!' Death by sabre-tooth tiger sounds a pretty awesome way to go, but taking the mindset of being cautious now in the modern world isn't just about avoiding death, it's about avoiding any kind of risk, which all too easily equates to misery, boredom and a life not fully lived.

The repercussions of a lack of confidence is often a state of stagnation, which can lead to a lack of activity, growth and development. Now this may not seem so severe or such a bad thing at first, but there's never enough times you can remind people around you about a sentence that changed my life; that *the opposite of happiness is boredom*. We should be in a constant fight to not be or feel stagnated, some people need reminding of that, and that we should be zealously going after things that make us uncomfortable and of course, the growth that comes with it.

'Be willing to be uncomfortable. Be comfortable being uncomfortable. It may get tough, but it's a small price to pay for living a dream.'

Peter McWilliams, author

Comfort and growth go hand in hand. There's a lot of cheesy bullshit on the internet about how pressure is what forms diamonds, I don't think you need reminding of that. I think if you ever want to check the pulse on your personal growth and development, the amount of comfort and discomfort in your life is a great place to look. Remember, just like growing muscle or developing your fitness, it's imperative you overreach frequently, not too much, not too little. But finding and hitting the sweet spot enables you to progress on and on to be a version of yourself that can quite literally do more than the version of you a short amount of time ago could ever accomplish.

Ask yourself what uncomfortable things you've put yourself through recently, then you can get an accurate gauge on how much you're developing and growing right now. If you're not challenging yourself, you're not developing yourself.

A Pyrrhic Mindset

A pyrrhic victory is a victory that inflicts such a devastating toll on the victor that it is tantamount to defeat. A pyrrhic victory takes a heavy toll that negates any true sense of achievement or damages long-term progress.

Why is this of importance? Because there are times that being confident enough to do something would be dire, futile and well, stupid. Imagine a dog leaping off a cliff to eat a bird. Not worth it. Imagine an orca getting beached chasing a seal pup. Again, although they may get their teeth into a seal pup, at what cost? Their own demise. However, this is the important thing to realise: pyrrhic victories are very rare and incredibly unlikely.

So when we think about what is on the line to lose in everyday life, the notion that the outcome would be tantamount to losing is so unlikely we're almost guaranteed a net positive outcome from it. Even if your boss declines a pay rise, the idea that you want one lives in their head rent free. Even if the person you approach is already in a relationship, you'll have made their day better (as long as you're polite doing so). Enquiring for a job, a position or even just putting yourself out there rarely comes at any loss. Utilising social media, albeit in some audacious demeanour, still puts you in a net positive position; even if some people don't agree or don't like what you have to say, you're still inching closer with actions than inactions. You must ask yourself, 'why do I not want to do this?' What is there to truly lose? If the outcome is not pyrrhic, then what truly do I have to lose? Often, nothing at all.

I really champion anyone to get behind a hobby or passion project: a podcast with your friends, a social media page for something that you find personally rewarding, or even taking evening classes to learn a new skill. Only a pyrrhic victory is not worth chasing. Anything where there is no downside should be exploited or at least tried. Especially if it makes you slightly uncomfortable, you can get and obtain the growth from such tasks without ever putting yourself in harm's way.

The Zeigarnik Effect

Is there a cost to inaction? Is there a true cost to not having the confidence to do certain things? I believe so. Let me introduce to you the Zeigarnik effect named after a Soviet psychologist called Bluma Zeigarnik. In psychology, the Zeigarnik effect occurs when an activity that has been interrupted may be more readily recalled or remembered. The original story comes after noticing that waiters can recollect an open order with much more clarity than a bill that has been paid already. The reason for this is that a task being established creates task-specific tension in the brain; this improves our ability to focus, remember and think about things we're doing. It was concluded by Bluma Zeigarnik that the tension is relieved on completion of the task. This is used with clickbait titles on social media and the internet. Let's for a moment think of an unfinished task as an 'open loop', when you finish that task it's now a 'closed loop'. So when you read a title saying '3 things your personal trainer never told you about losing fat!' a loop has been opened in your mind, you feel like you want it to be closed, the story is now living rent free in your mind and you know that if you click on that link you can get closure for your loop. This is also used on television before a break. 'Guys, coming up we have 11 ways to survive a zombie apocalypse from home, but first a quick advert break, see you in a few minutes.' Very cleverly the television presenters have opened a Zeigarnik loop before the adverts and the desire to close the loop will keep your attention to wait through the adverts. There's nothing worse than a cliffhanger, right? Waiting all the way to the end of the movie and it says, 'to be continued', the potential ending lives rent free in your mind so you'll be eagerly anticipating the sequel.

Forty college students participated in a study where they'd be asked to do a puzzle, then be given an amount of time to do it. Now the catch was that they would not be given enough time to finish it; 86 per cent of the students participating in the puzzle stayed on to finish it after the time ran out, despite there being no reward for their actions. (See References, p. 263)

So why am I bringing this to your attention? Because I have a feeling that not being confident in certain situations takes up our mental resources and those resources may be costly. Not being confident enough to ask something, to talk to someone, to enquire about a job or to say something that may not go down well inside your own mind: inaction creates an open loop, it then reminds our minds every day and these things compound. I'm building an argument to say that an action done (even if it fails) is a more positive outcome than no action at all, because failing at a task is a closed loop, you can put it behind you and go on about your day. It's been 'put to bed' so to speak. But the person you saw on the London Underground that locked eyes with you who you haven't got out of your mind all day, the one you were going to talk to? They're gone and you're still thinking about them, right? Ok, let's say you're in a loving relationship but there's a change you want to implement at work, you're not sure how they're going to take it, you're about to have your moment and let it all out, but at the very last moment you're afraid of the potential rejection, you say nothing and the loop is left open. If it doesn't get closed, how long will it take up your mental resources? I believe that closing loops whenever they open means more mental resources to other important tasks. Mark Manson, one of my favourite authors, experienced something similar when he said that getting married to him meant that his brain freed up a huge amount of resources from not having to worry about who he was going to marry and spend his life with. Getting married to him closed a rather substantial loop in his mind, allowing him to focus on more important stuff.

So, I'd like to ask you, what loops do you have left open through inaction? I love the saying that 'bad news is better than no news'. In this scenario as much as others, it's so important we take action when opportunities present themselves so that we can close loops and keep our mind free for much more productive thoughts than the things we didn't do.

Cognitive Biases

In short, there are some biases that we as human beings tend to make. I've spoken about them before in my previous books: the sunk cost fallacy, loss aversion, pessimism biases. Don't worry, I'll be covering these off with their relation to confidence in this book. But one of the main reasons I want to make you knowledgeable about them is that I believe there is an element of bullet-proofing that we can do for your mind and beliefs as you understand them. If these can enable a bit of clarity and ownership of your decisions, then hopefully you're destined to make better choices moving forward.

The Self-Serving Bias

Imagine the scenario: I set you a test to do today, you absolutely nailed it, you got the best score out of everyone you know. The reason? Well, you did the work, you did the research, you put your mind to it and you crushed it, well done you. Ok, three weeks from now, I get you to do another and it goes terribly. Why? Well, maybe it was that bad night's sleep? There's been a lot on your mind and you're extra busy this time of year. What is going on here? The self-serving bias is when you succeed, you give yourself all the credit that is due, but when you fail at a task you look for external factors to blame. It's almost a programmed way of letting yourself off for not performing or completing tasks as you should have. I can recall this any time I've played *Call of Duty* online. Should I perform really well, it's because I'm a brilliant player, should I do badly it's usually 'bullshit' or the internet connection must have lagged, someone must be cheating and that's why I lost.

The self-serving bias I feel is a problem for a lot of people; if we do not take responsibility and ownership for our mistakes and failures then we do not learn from them. Not learning from our mistakes is going to make it incredibly difficult to stop making them in the future. I'm sure shouting 'bullshit' every five minutes on my PlayStation is not too much of a problem, except for my neighbours wishing I'd shout it a bit quieter. But when things do go wrong and mistakes are made, we need to learn from them. Mistakes are like steering slightly in the wrong direction on a boat, it's not about just saying, 'well, this boat has terrible navigation', it's about making slight changes to correct the course with every learning opportunity.

If people are unable to correlate their own failures with their own mistakes, they're going to have an incredibly difficult time improving themselves. From being introspective with thinking why things haven't served us all the way, to clever marketing like A/B split tests. Let's say you start a business selling your favourite type of t-shirt. On the days you make good sales you may think you're an excellent salesperson, but the self-serving bias may interfere on poor sales days, you may conclude 'oh, the weather is good', that's why no one bought my product today. But by being introspective with your thoughts surrounding something not going well, we can put things into practice. I suffer personally with the self-serving bias, especially in relationships and work life. The A/B split testing is something I do more and more when I suspect I'm succumbing to the self-serving bias. So if a sales page of my own isn't doing well, I'll create multiple sales pages: the original, one with less text, one with more and perhaps one with a video and split the traffic to the pages evenly. If the 'control' page scores the best, maybe it was the weather that accounted for shitty sales, but all too often that's not the case. The data shows it's what I'm doing that's at fault, not external circumstances that are much easier to blame.

Escalation of Commitment

I know this can seem like the sunk cost fallacy repackaged from my last book; where people remain invested in certain things not because it's the right thing to do, but because of what they have already invested in it. To summarise, it's why you're going to make it to the end of the book you're not enjoying. You read the first third and it's still not great, but you're going to keep going so that it doesn't feel like you let the time reading it go to waste. It's one of the most impactful things I've ever written about. Sometimes, it's not just merely confidence we need in a situation. You may be sitting reading this thinking, 'I wish I had the confidence to leave my partner.' Or 'I wish I had the confidence to get out of a job I don't enjoy.' But I think it's important to arm you to understand the bias that perhaps is underlying to make you feel like you're not confident enough to make the change you want to … yet.

You got into a job because well, you needed a job, right? You stay there a while, you found it difficult at first but then as time goes on it becomes a bit easier and soon you know everyone, your routine is set, alarm goes off, you know the traffic off by heart. Over a few years you climb the ladder, dig in and persevere despite one elephant in the room that haunts you every hour of every day. You find yourself sat on a toilet lid staring at the clothes peg on the back of the door several times a day escaping your colleagues and the realisation stares you straight back in the face. *You don't like your job.* One of the issues we face is misinterpreting whether what we're doing is 'working for us'. Because if you think that getting paid equates to our lives working out, that is similar to thinking just because you and your partner live together in the same building that your relationship is 'working out'. As mentioned before when speaking about the sunk cost fallacy, it's not smart to remain invested in something purely based on what you've already invested into it. To select unhappiness over uncertainty isn't a recipe for a good life. I know people value consistency, but that isn't a tangible reason to remain in an endeavour that's not suiting you or making you happy. Human beings can be very stubborn, myself especially. I can find myself even slipping and remaining invested in things just so money doesn't go to waste. I started watching a film the other day, it's not great but I feel I have to finish it because of two biases together. The Zeigarnik effect is in play because the unfinished film has been left as an open loop. Then escalation of commitment/sunk cost fallacy has me by the balls thinking I should finish the film because I've already invested 90 minutes into the film, I don't want that going to waste, do I? Again, this is not a reason to remain in the endeavour, the time is lost, it's 'sunk' in fact and I won't get it back. This doesn't just exist within our professional lives and our relationships. This plays a massive role within financial decision making. Say you and your friend create an app you think is going to take off, you're told it will cost $40,000, so you invest $40,000 of savings into it and so far have nothing to show, then your app developers say with another $30,000 that they can get it ready. Do you admit defeat, or do you lean towards the idea that you've come this far and you may as well keep going? You'd need to ensure that the decision was a business decision and not an emotional decision based on your previous investment. You may have been told that you should invest your money into cryptocurrency just before it started declining heavily in May 2022. You're left with the decision of remaining invested because of what you've already put in, or making a rational decision to pull your money out because this investment strategy is clearly not working.

I wrote about why I hate the lottery in *Not A Life Coach* and I feel that even my parents succumb to the escalation of commitment with every single lottery ticket they purchase. They're more likely to die from a falling airplane part than they are to win the jackpot. Yet they've been doing it for years and there's no stopping them. Why? Because there is an emotional investment in every previous purchase, despite winning only a couple of pounds back here and there. They've been doing the lottery for so long, it seems a shame to let that go to waste by stopping now. Escalation of Commitment 1 My Parents 0.

As far as managing the escalation of commitment, I think it best to perhaps seek advice from someone or several people who have less of an emotional connection to the previous investment (or person, or job) and see what they have to say about it. Just know that your decisions will be tainted with your previous investment. I've had countless people come up to me and thank me from reading my first books that enabled them to realise they were only with their partners because of the previous investment into their partner; they blindly overlooked the fact the relationship didn't serve them anymore.

The Dunning-Kruger Effect

The Dunning-Kruger effect came to light in 1999 when David Dunning and Justin Kruger observed why people with very little experience in their field can be very overconfident. Unlike what we've just discussed, this can result in a kind of false sense of confidence when it comes to making certain decisions or assertions, and is interesting to consider within the framework of how our mindset can change depending on how significant or life-changing we feel the decision in hand to be.

'People tend to hold overly favourable views of their abilities in many social and intellectual domains. The authors suggest that this overestimation occurs, in part, because people who are unskilled in these domains suffer a dual burden: Not only do these people reach erroneous conclusions and make unfortunate choices, but their incompetence robs them of the metacognitive ability to realize it.' (See References, p. 263)

This effect is a hypothetical cognitive bias stating that people with low ability at a task overestimate their own ability, and that people with high ability at a task underestimate their own ability.

I've noticed this quite often in the sport of Brazilian jiu-jitsu, you always seem to find a cocky white belt who thinks he is ready to take the world on. In case you didn't know, the belts go in ascending level from white, blue, purple, brown and black, each on average about

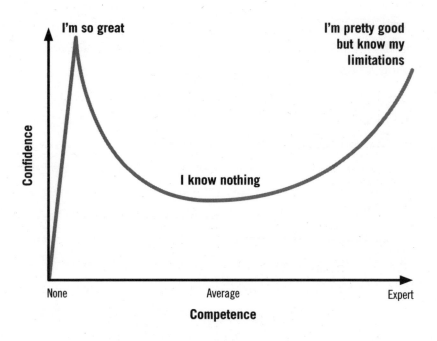

2 years of training at least to be awarded. At the time of writing this book, I'm a purple belt – coming up to 5 years of training so nearly halfway to black belt should I keep injuries at bay. So why is it when white belts somehow have this ingrained confidence so early on with such limited knowledge of the sport? Why do so many white belts end up having this unknockable confidence when they begin the sport? Well in short, **they don't know quite how much they don't know.**

If we draw back to my theory of previous experiences we could also conclude that someone new to a martial art hasn't taken many beatings in their life. Again, without pre-existing experiences of what it's like to be beaten and to be humbled would only spur on a strong sense of confidence. Very often a white belt hasn't been too widely exposed to much talent, only peers of the same belt level and same ability. Being in that environment could perhaps increase someone's confidence to a higher degree than being exposed to higher belts who would give them very different experiences earlier on. It's worth noting we do tend to keep the white belts grouped together, as they can unknowingly be rather dangerous. The famous saying goes, 'A white belt with good intentions causes more injuries to his training partners than any black belt with bad intentions.'

I would assume some of you reading this would have already in your lives come across someone mentioning the Dunning-Kruger effect. I use it often as a joke to put someone down as a form of banter, especially in training if a friend of mine who has never done jiu-jitsu says, 'I'm going to get you in an armbar next time we roll in jiu-jitsu.' I'll smirk back and say, 'Ah, the old Dunning-Kruger effect in action!' It's a good way to get inside anyone's head you want to wind up. If they ask, 'What is that?', you'll be able to answer confidently, 'Oh, you didn't know? It's a phenomenon within the realm of overconfidence.' You can come out on top of the intellect hierarchy in the conversation. Every day is a school day, right?

This effect has faced some rebuttal over the years. I've been down some deep rabbit holes of blogs, papers, articles and found a lot of people who disagree with how we perceive the effect. In his article 'The Dunning-Kruger Effect Is Probably Not Real' for the McGill Office for Science and Society, Jonathan Jarry writes:

'The most important mistake people make about the Dunning-Kruger effect, according to Dr Dunning, has to do with who falls victim to it. "The effect is about us, not them," he wrote to me. "The lesson of the effect was always about how we should be humble and cautious about ourselves." The Dunning-Kruger effect is not about dumb people. It's mostly about all of us when it comes to things we are not very competent at.

'In a nutshell, **the Dunning-Kruger effect was originally defined as a bias in our thinking**. If I am terrible at English grammar and am told to answer a quiz testing my knowledge of English grammar, this bias in my thinking would lead me, according to the theory, to believe I would get a higher score than I actually would. And if I excel at English grammar, the effect dictates I would be likely to slightly underestimate how well I would do. I might predict I would get a 70% score while my actual score would be 90%. But if my actual score was 15% (because I'm terrible at grammar), I might think more highly of myself and predict a score of 60%. This discrepancy is the effect, and it is thought to be due to a specific problem with our brain's ability to assess its skills.'

'Dr Dunning tells me he believes the effect "has more to do with being misinformed rather than uninformed". If I am asked the boiling point of mercury, it is clear my brain does not hold the answer. But if I am asked what is the capital of Scotland, I may think I know enough to say Glasgow, but it turns out it's Edinburgh. That's misinformation and it's pushing down on that confidence button in my brain.' (See References, p. 263)

From what I find anywhere I read up on the topic, it's clear to me there is a narrative here that this effect is not about saying or implying that stupid people are stupid; this is not a finger-pointing effect whereby we call out people for being idiots or imply that anyone new to something is going to be overconfident (unless in a context of good banter). This is more about an internal narrative that perhaps you don't know as much as you may think you do, especially at the outset; it's about proceeding with caution in your early days as there is a human tendency to overestimate one's abilities. I know for a fact when I passed my driving test, within a few months at 17 years old I thought I was one of the best drivers on the road. So where does this overconfidence stem from? Is this poor cognitive programming, is it the Dunning-Kruger effect or could it have something to do with the 'M' word that we talked about? (See p. 45 on manifestation.)

Heuristics

I first came across this word in Daniel Kahneman's book *Thinking, Fast and Slow*. I had absolutely no idea what it meant. Heuristics make decisions as fast as possible by simplifying information not for the best solution, but instead, for what the fastest solution would be for human needs. So I'll give you some examples. For instance, estimating how far away something is. I'd employ a heuristic tactic like 'how many football pitches could I fit lengthways between me and that thing?' I know that a football pitch is roughly 100 metres in length, so I think how many could fit between me and there, two and a half? It's roughly 250 metres away; it's not an optimal means of measuring a distance but it can be utilised to speed up the process of finding a satisfactory solution. Another thing I love is that I know a litre of water weighs a kilogram, so then I know that a can of Coke weighs 330 g, it's 330 ml right? So if I need to guess what 100 g feels like, I pick something up and think in my mind how heavy it is relative to a can of Coke. It's not an accurate science, but if it feels more like a half-full can, I can be fairly sure it's over 150 g.

Other heuristics by name that you'll have previous knowledge of would be 'trial and error', 'a rule of thumb' or an 'educated guess'.

The Availability Heuristic Bias

Also known as the 'availability bias', this is a mental shortcut the brain makes in determining something using only information that is available at the time. If you can think of several examples of something happening, you'll assume it to be true. For instance, if you watch the news a lot, or scroll social media, you'll probably think being a police officer is a pretty dangerous or risky job. You'll have seen countless articles and stories about police shootings, you've seen it all over the news. But the truth is, being a roofer is much more dangerous as a profession than being a police officer, with a fatal injury rate of 47.0 out of 100,000. Whereas as a police officer in the United States of America, the fatality rate is 13.4 out of 100,000. (See References, p. 263)

In a similar way, we're led to believe nuclear power is really dangerous, because of catastrophes such as Chernobyl, Ukraine in 1986. But there are more deaths associated with roofers putting up solar panels each year than nuclear power related deaths. Studies based on World Health Organisation data and other sources found that globally, about 100 people die for each terawatt-hour of electricity produced by coal, 36 from oil, 4 from natural gas, 0.44 for rooftop solar and 0.04 from nuclear. (See References, p. 263) I know this is a confidence book, but I wanted to bring to your attention our tendency to misinterpret reality based on what we've been exposed to, not what has been available to us before the decision-making process.

Should a plane crash, we completely lose sight of planes being one of the safest means of travel. When a tragic and fatal shark attack occurs off the coast of Australia, we lose sight of the fact we're more likely to die in a car accident on the way to the beach than we are to be bitten in the sea. I commonly remind people that they are much more likely to take their own lives than lose it in the sea to a great white shark, another stern reminder to ensure mental health is prioritised above all else in life. If that's too morbid, instead think that when you swim in the sea you're much more likely to drown than you are to be bitten or eaten.

> 'Nothing in life is as important as you think it is,
> while you are thinking about it.'
>
> Daniel Kahneman, *Thinking, Fast and Slow*

The reason I talk about this bias is to draw attention to the reality that your thoughts and decisions are based largely upon what you are exposed to, the media you watch and the people you surround yourself with, much more than you realise. You'll make decisions based on what is available to you, not necessarily what is true. This is another reason to really be selective with whom and what you surround yourself with. Don't underestimate the impact of naysayers and the news. The facts and reality about something being possible are much higher than what you may believe; your mind's mental shortcuts could be alluding that your ambitions are much less likely than they really are. The human mind is fantastic, but it's not always to be trusted. I can flip this both ways: if people had never seen a lottery winner on TV, their 1 in 300 million chances of winning wouldn't seem so realistic. (See References, p. 263) People hugely overestimate their personal probability of winning the lottery, and as long as the lottery organisers keep reminding people of their chances of winning and not their chances of losing, they'll remain in business.

I'll leave some fun facts for you to bring up when the conversation next arises and you can become the smart arse of your friendship group:

- Driving the same distance as a flight is 65 times more risky than flying it. (See References, p. 263)
- Risk of shark attack is one in 3.7 million.
- You're around 47 times more likely to be hit by lightning than bitten by a shark. (See References, p. 263)

Don't forget, the amount of media you expose yourself to has a tremendous impact on what you believe to be true because of the availability heuristic bias.

The Confidence Heuristic

According to the confidence heuristic, people are confident when they think or know they are right, and their confidence makes them persuasive. (See References, p. 263) Imagine you're sitting with two friends having a coffee, and you need to get to the other part of town for a work meeting. You ask your two friends which way they think is faster, through the city or around via the coast. Your first friend says, 'Errrm, through the city could be busy around this time, I'm not sure, I think you may be better going the coastal way.' You turn to your other friend and they say confidently, 'Oh, the coastal way is so much faster, you're for sure better off going that way.' It goes without saying the second friend is much more convincing, it makes their information seem more legitimate because, well, they're confident about it. This is something that's rife on social media: it's not what people are saying necessarily but how they're saying it that makes people so drawn-in to what they're saying.

I think you'd struggle to create something like a cult without a confident leader. If you're unaware of the persuasive powers that someone confident can possess, I'll bring you back in time to one of the most bizarre happenings of the twentieth century. On 26 March 1997, deputies of the San Diego County Sheriff's Department discovered the bodies of the 39 active members of what was soon to be named the 'Heaven's Gate' religious group. They had participated in a mass suicide, coinciding with the closest approach of comet Hale–Bopp. The members were convinced that the earth was soon to be 'recycled' and that there was a spaceship on the soon approaching comet. Several of the members went through voluntary castrations before having a last supper together. (See References, p. 263) This is just one of many bizarre examples of the persuasion confidence can have when people believe so strongly in something. This ties me into the next topic which is incredibly important when it comes to understanding confidence; that next topic is overconfidence.

Overconfidence

'Human beings are over confidence machines.'

David Brooks, *The Social Animal*

When I think about the root or the source of the human ability to be so overconfident, I think it must have been an evolutionary trait. I like to remind people that when we look at planet earth, we should not see it as all of nature or the natural world, and then humans existing separately alongside it. We are a part of nature, we are mammals living in the same kingdom as the rest of all living animals. We are not unique, we're merely just technologically advanced due to many factors, most important of which are opposable thumbs, good eyesight and large brains. If it was not for the human tendency to be overconfident, we'd not see people climb to the summit of Mount Everest, astronauts on the moon or simple everyday things we probably take for granted like the lightbulb. If Thomas Edison hadn't been overconfident, he may have given up on his thousandth attempt, but he didn't. Since I mentioned Mount Everest, I think this chapter is a great place to mention a sign I saw outside a pub once. It said on the outside 'Every corpse on Mount Everest was once a highly motivated person, calm down and come inside for a beer.' I thought that was some of the finest signage I'd ever seen in my life.

Overconfidence is coined to be a negative thing by most people, I'm sure if I was to interview people on the street and ask if over-confidence was an attractive feature, they'd say no, they'd think it meant cocky or arrogant. But somewhere through human evolution we must have evolved overconfident people to sail across oceans, climb over treacherous terrain and even go to war. Sometimes too many people can be overconfident, for instance two generals with opposing armed forces the night before battle would expect their army to win; if they didn't think it was possible to win, they'd more than likely surrender.

I bet as you read this chapter you're thinking, 'not me, I'm not over-confident, not in the slightest', right? But one thing I can tell you even though chances are we haven't met is that you're a pretty good driver, right? Above average for sure. It's been shown that 93 per cent of drivers from the United States think their 'driving skills' are above average when it comes to driving. (See References, p. 263) Well, this is for a few reasons, one in particular is what people deem 'driving skills'. My mum would say she has great 'driving skills' because she never goes above the speed limit, whereas I may say that I have the best 'driving skills' as I could arrive at the destination before her and parallel park without curbing the alloy wheels as she's well known for doing in the Smith household. The field of how good a driver people think they are, is actually quite well studied, but you know something is wrong when 93 per cent of people think they're above average, that's quite impossible because the average is supposed to be the mean of all data. This isn't the only field in which people are often overconfident. Financially people are also overconfident, this is why we have mortgage insurance and thorough investigation of whether or not people can actually afford to borrow money. After the collapse of the housing market in 2008, perhaps people's confidence has been better aligned with what they can really afford. Interestingly, most people report that they are better eyewitnesses than the rest of the population. Faulty eyewitness testimony has been implicated in at least 75 per cent of DNA exoneration cases – more than any other cause. (See References, p. 263)

Overcompensation confidence is something we can spot a mile off. This is where someone externally tries so hard to portray confidence to cover up their insecurities. For instance, think about people who try to convince you that they're rich, especially those really annoying watch poses, they personally do my head in. You'll see in every picture they have, they use the opportunity to get the dial of the watch to face the camera. We get it, you're wearing an expensive watch. The same person who poses in front of their car for Instagram clout. From what I have observed in life, those who truly have the riches don't feel the incessant need to prove to you that they're rich. Within the world of confidence this is also something that I see. People who aren't confident try to overcompensate by proving their confidence by dressing a certain way or acting in a certain manner.

Overconfidence isn't unique to just our genetics and our evolutionary pathways where 'fortune favours the brave' as the famous Latin proverb goes. It can all too easily stem from biases we have and the way we interpret data, and one that I think about a lot in my field of work is the survivorship bias.

The Survivorship Bias

Abraham Wald is the name of the mathematician who was given the task of finding a solution to armouring planes in World War II. He would have to collate data on where the planes were being damaged (see below). (See References, p. 263)

The military bosses instructed Wald to armour the planes in the places where they were receiving the most damage, according to the data. Then Wald famously replied:

'What you should do is reinforce the area around the motors and the cockpit. You should remember that the worst-hit planes never come back. All the data we have come from planes that make it to the bases. You don't see that the spots with no damage are the worst places to be hit because these planes never come back.' (See References, p. 263)

This is the survivorship bias in full effect. Another example I absolutely love is from UK-based illusionist Derren Brown. In one of his TV 'stunts' he showed the nation a system for perfectly predicting what

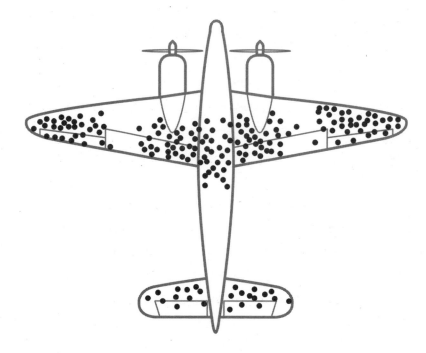

horse would win in a race. The TV production anonymously text a single mother named 'Khadisha' and she's instructed on which horse will win a specific race. After 5 wins where she's consecutively bet more money each turn, she's invited to a racecourse to meet Derren Brown to understand 'the system'. He meets her at the racecourse and on TV you find out she's literally scraped everything she could pull together, including borrowing money from friends to bet £4,000 ($7,115 AUD).

The system turned out to be as simple as messaging thousands of people with different horse race predictions. After the first five horse races, 80 per cent of people dropped out when their horse lost, 20 per cent remained and so forth until the last person left as a survivor of thousands of betting attempts was Khadisha. That's a classic portrayal of the survivorship bias in action. Should we ask Khadisha about the system, her position and standpoint on the 'system' is biased because she's a survivor, a lucky anomaly. As time goes on and her bias strengthens, others diminish to zero as they're disqualified over time when their horse ultimately doesn't finish the race. Similar to the planes that never returned home from the war, and whose data couldn't contribute to Abraham Wald's findings. So, when we're looking at confidence, we must almost put a lens on our findings to interpret any biases that could influence this. I've battled with survivorship bias myself with any mentoring I've done to other business owners over the years. Are the systems I have used truly effective or am I stood in the position of the survivor? Perhaps there are hundreds, even thousands of people who have used the exact same principles, but here I am holding the last betting ticket to the horse race through the odds of luck. It's not about tearing down someone's own belief of their success, but instead to have the clarity to put your hands up and understand that the survivorship bias can be a tremendously influential factor in success. It could keep you straight, humble and enable you to have clarity in the world of the fine line between confidence and overconfidence.

The survivorship bias is commonly seen in any casino you go to. In fact, Las Vegas is built on a fantastic mix of overconfidence and survivorship bias coexisting together. Think about when someone says 'the table is hot'. This means that the players on this table are winning. Now, I'm not sure if you're aware but the house always wins. Every single game in a casino is leaning towards the house, the casino. Blackjack has the best odds of winning, with a house edge of just 1 per cent in most casinos. (See References, p. 263) With every win, you survive another random draw of skill and luck. With each win your confidence increases even though the odds remain the same. We all have those friends who portray themselves as almost professional gamblers, but there again is a confirmation bias within their own minds where every time they win they take note of their exceptional gambling skills, whereas when they lose it's no doubt external forces. The internal self-serving bias can then blame the table or the 'shitty hand' you were dealt. People can and do walk away from tables being up, but eventually it will come back to bite them. The casino is the home of biases; when someone does win a slot machine's prize (which is one of the most unlikely) the casino will make a big fuss about it so other people think, 'That could be me!' If you want to see the survivorship bias in full action, ask someone who left Las Vegas a winner how they did it. They will be like Khadisha in the Derren Brown TV show, one survivor among a sea of losers.

I'm a firm believer in the idea that people create their own luck. 'The harder I practise, the luckier I get' was famously said by the South

African golfer Gary Player. But there is always going to be an element of chance in this game, and it doesn't take much of an advantage to get ahead. Don't overlook your chance and your luck and assume it's your greatness instead – that's ego, not confidence.

> *'Society rewards overconfidence.'*
>
> Daniel Kahneman, *Thinking, Fast and Slow*

In leadership, good coaching or setting up a new business, it's rewarding to be overconfident. Whether you're a coach telling your team they're going to win today, a leader bringing his country together to overcome adversity or a meeting between soon to be business partners talking about how their new idea is going to be the biggest thing ever, this is the rewarding and sometimes essential element of overconfidence that's required to predict success and then to accomplish success.

Imagine if you will that you're taking your new business onto *Dragons' Den*, the popular TV show where you have to pitch your business for investment to leaders in the investorship scene. You need to gleam with confidence about your business, your pitch and your position. Your predictions of revenue must be confident, you don't pitch your low-end margins. You don't stand there saying, 'Errm, well it could on a good year do this.' You need to inspire whoever you're talking to that it can and will do the very best possible. This doesn't mean to falsify the numbers, but surely to select the highest echelon of possible predictions. If I had to select someone for a job role, given they all have even experience and qualifications, chances are I'd reward the most confident with a job.

For muscles to develop stronger and bigger, there needs to be a certain amount of overreaching, where they're pushed to new boundaries they've not been before. This is a similar exercise to what I believe we need to do with overconfidence, seeing and believing that it's truly possible. The way Jeff Bezos was when he set up Amazon from his garage. The same thing you would do when you've been lifting the same weight for a while; it's time to slide two small discs on to either end of the barbell and see what you're truly capable of. If you don't believe your dreams are possible, the path to accomplishing them looks a lot less likely. Whatever team gets promoted to the Premier League, whether it be rugby, football or netball, it is the role of the coaches to set the sights on winning the league, or finishing within the top 3, to ignore the naysayers and to actually accomplish it.

I'm not the biggest fan of football, but Leicester City Football Club in 2015–16 played a part in what can only be described as one of the greatest sporting stories of all time. In only their second season back in the Premier League, Leicester City won the title on 2 May 2016 against odds the bookmakers set at 5,000–1 before the season kicked off. (See References, p. 263)

What do you think was the mentality or attitude within the side? To just do alright? To survive? To not get relegated? There would have been a sense of overconfidence, to be the underdog and to go for it without compromise. This isn't a cocky attitude, it's a perfect combination of audacity and aspiration based on your existing knowledge and skill set, executed perfectly. How Leicester City managed to secure so many wins, I believe, wasn't just to do with how prepared they were for the season. I played rugby for 15 years and let me tell you this: it's the teams that are the underdogs that you need to keep an eye on. Bottom of the league would be cornered, top of the league comfortable. The underdog has nothing to lose in most cases. Proving people wrong is one of the best motivators possible.

Let's move on to one of the most powerful tools anyone can have, I call it the 'Underdog Mindset'.

The Underdog Mindset

I think that one of the best advantages you can have in life is not to be favourite. I think with that comes a fantastic mentality where you do not have the expectations or pressures that someone who is favourite would have. I've been in a position of underdog for much of my career. As a personal trainer I didn't have the sheer experience, nor the physique of many of my competitors, which made me an underdog and in turn more motivated to grow my brand and businesses beyond theirs. As an author too, I knew deep down when I released my first book that people would assume it was ghost written, where a professional writer would make it look like it was mine and write it for me, which is common practice for many people these days. I knew that I was coming into the realm of book writing as an underdog, people not thinking I could write or put in the time or effort necessary to be successful as an author and to be honest, I love the feeling of being the unlikely favourite.

The dictionary definition of the underdog is 'the person or team considered to be the weakest and the least likely to win'.

> *'The wolf on the hill is not as hungry as the wolf climbing the hill.'*
>
> Arnold Schwarzenegger

Being at the top of your 'hill' can make you weak, I believe. Winning too much can make you weak, which is why I think it's important that whatever realm you exist in, you never see yourself at the top, or on the top of the hill. Our perceptions of our situation, whether personal, financial or professional are subjectively held in our minds, and I think back to the adage that says, 'If you're the smartest in the room, you're in the wrong room'. We constantly need to reset the boundaries or desires to higher and further peaks to avoid being the 'top dog' and instead try to remain permanently the underdog in whatever realm we choose. This is an imperative point in mindset, that you look forward to the top of the 'hill' and not to behind you or beside you. The 'blinkers on' mentality of moving forward is essential to progress, not worrying about what's on your tail but instead how to progress to the peak that only ever gets further away the higher you climb.

One of the most powerful and important parts of the underdog mentality is to do with expectations. Expectations you should hold to yourself and hold yourself accountable to. When the numbers or the data points in the direction that you won't win, that you can't do it. This is the fuel the mind needs to try to prove everyone wrong and the best part is that everyone loves an underdog. So whether it's punching high for a new promotion, whether it's being bold to ask someone out or setting out to begin a business. Proving the naysayers wrong is what helps you pull yourself out of bed in the morning when your alarm says, 'get up' but your body says, 'lie in'. When I first became a personal trainer, I had my closest friends say, 'Don't do it, everyone is doing it and you can't do well as a personal trainer.' I'd be lying if I said that didn't get me out of bed some days, in front of the camera on others, and stepping on stage at events to prove their words wrong.

Another time I found a similar experience was when a player got sent off in rugby. You'd expect the other team to have a true advantage, but it's not the case as often as you'd think. As you see your teammate sent off, you know deep down you have to cover their part of the team for the next 10 minutes. You know you're going to have to tackle harder, run further and work at a much more intense pace to ensure success. This is an observation known as social loafing. Social loafing is the perceived psychological phenomenon that team members do less in a group setting. (See References, p. 263) One of the first experiments in social loafing was conducted by French agricultural engineer, Max Ringelmann in 1913. He asked participants to pull on a rope both alone and in groups. He found that when people were part of a group, they made less of an effort to pull the rope than they did when working individually. (See References, p. 263) When we know that other people are there to take the slack, we don't work as hard. This is a big issue with big organisations and companies that hire too many people without creating sub-divisions to keep accountability. Let's be honest, we're never working at full capacity, ever. We always can do more, and that's not some bullshit wake up at 4 a.m. every day nonsense that gurus are always going on about. But instead that, should we hit the wall, we can dig deeper, find more drive and do better. Like the phenomenon of a player being sent off and the team performing better. So, you can imagine when the top of the league turns up to the bottom of the league in rugby, like I said before. If every player only turns up at 85 per cent effort each, that's 15 per cent (x 15) = 225 per cent missing effort, which is worse than two players being sent off. It's the mindset of the team, just as much as anything else, that counts.

I have my entire career put myself up against people much more successful than I am, not to demotivate myself, but instead to always feel like my back is up against it. To go back to the adage of the wolf and the hill, my hill is a forever changing landscape where I am the underdog climbing it every day. It makes the inevitability of failing a lot easier to handle and manage. It's not a motivational means for everyone, but personally I prefer it.

It's clear we're all different when driven towards success and how we see the motivations that we face every day. The desire to be an underdog is a strange desire, so why is it that some people desire winning so much, when others are quite happy just to take part?

Competitiveness

Why are some people so competitive compared to others? Whether being the youngest in a big family, having siblings to compete with through childhood and adolescence it's clear some people are more competitive than others. Competition between organisms is biology, it's evolution in fact. There are a finite and limited sum of resources that organisms fight for. Being competitive I believe can help people work harder towards their goals. Not everyone knows they're even in the race, one young person may be desperate to have more followers than their friend for no other reason than seeing it as a competitive space to be victorious. The other friend may not even know they're in a competition, I called this 'the invisible race' in *Not a Life Coach*. I'm fiercely competitive with people who I seek inspiration from. A large majority of them don't even know I exist let alone that I'm competing with them. I think fierce competitiveness is great for confidence, I think a lot

107

of people have it deep down inside them but many people suppress it like it's a negative trait.

When you think of it, what arrogance is to confidence is what being Machiavellian is to competitiveness. (Machiavellians are sly, deceptive, distrusting, and manipulative.) When you find the sweet spot I think it's an incredible trait to have. I think we are all guilty of associating competitiveness with success, but I think that's the wrong way to look at it. Competitiveness is our relationship with failing over and over again, not because we fear failure, but to feed our incessant need and requirements to be successful, to compete and to win. I think every reader of this book should champion their inner competitive spirit and bring it out. I like to play chess with my girlfriend whilst we cook dinner or when we're on flights, we play tennis often and we're fiercely competitive. I think it's not only a good mindset for life, but within relationships too and other situations from managing small groups to incentivising employees.

It's not essential you're the most competitive person in the room, but becoming competitive may just be the key you can use to unlock more confidence. This works well if you and someone else share a common hindrance in the realm of confidence. Perhaps two personal trainers could see who can book the most consultations in a day, two sales people compete for the most sales, two single friends could see who can organise the most dates with strangers in a week and so forth. When competition takes over the mind, a lack of confidence is often left behind. Winning isn't just part of human nature, it's part of all nature.

Chapter 4

Fear

'We suffer more often in imagination than in reality.'

L A Seneca, Roman philosopher

What is the true root of poor confidence? Is it fear? If we look to the opposing end of the spectrum from confidence, I think we all find fear. Confidence is what degrades and disappears after we let fear take control of our thoughts, our logic and our judgements. Should you be consumed too much by fear, there won't be much space left for confidence. This could all too well leave people feeling like they 'don't have confidence', but could it be more likely that they just have too much fear governing their thoughts and predicting their outcomes?

From an evolutionary standpoint fear is crucial to survival, to be risk averse and to ensure the continuation of your lineage, sure. But in the modern world, what is it we fear? Rejection? To look stupid? To not get the job? To not get the person's number? To lack fear when being in the vicinity of a sabre-tooth tiger 20,000 years ago could mean death, I appreciate that. But the world we live in is safer than ever; the majority of things we fear are not worthy of such fear. Crippling insecurities to speak publicly, fear of rejection to talk to a stranger, the astounding bias to expect the worst-case scenario instead of the best. Our fear response in our minds hasn't evolved as fast as we have. It was only a few thousand years ago that we had a legitimate reason to fear the animal kingdom. Hyenas, snakes, Komodo dragons and even carnivorous kangaroos. (See References, p. 263) Think about it, what's your biggest fear today? That you didn't charge your laptop last night before you went to work or the train may be delayed? Ok, that's a fairly flippant one, but you get the point.

When looking at the dictionary we see that 'fear is the most general term and implies anxiety and usually loss of courage'. I like the way it's termed as a loss of courage, almost as if we have it and we only lose it if we choose to. Inaction, I believe, is coupled with fear more so than confidence. People may not use social media for their business as a **fear** of judgement, people may not ask someone for their number through **fear** of rejection, people may not want to object to the status quo through **fear** of exclusion and people may not quit their jobs to pursue their passions through **fear** of failure.

In Ryan Holiday's most recent book about courage, he mentions a quote from Ulysses S Grant that has really resonated with me. This is from the chapter 'There are always more before they are counted' in *Courage is Calling – Fortune Favours the Brave*:

'The prairie grass was tall and we could not see the beasts, but the sound indicated that they were near. To my ear it appeared that there must have been enough of them to devour our party, horses and all, at a single meal. He understood the nature of the animal and the capacity of a few to make believe there was an unlimited number of them.

'He kept on towards the noise, unmoved. I followed in his trail, lacking moral courage to turn back and join our sick companion. "Grant, how many wolves do you think there are in that pack?" Knowing where he was from, and suspecting that he thought I would overestimate the number, I determined to show my acquaintance with the animal by putting the estimate below what possibly could be correct, and answered: "Oh, about twenty," very indifferently.

'He smiled and rode on. In a minute we were close upon them, and before they saw us. There were just TWO of them. Seated upon their haunches, with their mouths close together, they had made all the noise we had been hearing for the past ten minutes.' (See References, p. 263)

This short snippet from a much longer story really resonated with me because many of our fears in reality are not that scary at all. It's the perpetuating nature of our mind that multiplies and grows our fears to make them bigger and more daunting as they go. It's only when we can objectively count or measure our fears that we can realise how much our mind when left to itself can multiply our fears at an almost exponential rate. The process isn't always as simple as merely counting, as not all fears are numerical. The lesson to be learned from the story is more to do with the idea that until you know for sure the extent of something being fearful, you should try not to worry about it as much as your mind will want to. You'll build up your opponent in your mind and place yourself second as human nature. Whether it's someone else applying for the same job, your partner's ex or your opponent in martial arts. There are always more until they are counted. George St

Pierre, one of the best mixed martial artists of all time, said he was absolutely petrified before every single one of his fights. Except one, he said, the only fight he had where he didn't have a poor night's sleep and a twist in his stomach, he lost. 'Before every fight, before every training session, I was scared. I was afraid that someone would beat me, the fear that I would disappoint my mentor, and the fear that someone would hurt me. I even thought I wasn't made for this.' That's coming from one of the most decorated UFC fighters of all time. The fear is normal, courage comes from continuing the path. So do not think that you're entitled to a journey without fear around every corner. Instead, understand that fear is an essential part of the process; the courage comes from stepping towards the fear head on, ready for anything. Even losing.

> 'The obstacles, the enemies, the critics – they are not as numerous as you think. It's an illusion they want you to believe.'
>
> Ryan Holiday, *Courage is Calling*

Fear of Failure

> 'A man cannot be comfortable without his own approval.'
>
> Mark Twain

If we were to ask the majority of people who use a personal trainer why they use a personal trainer, I can imagine a huge amount of people would say, 'I'm worried I'd do something wrong if I didn't.' There are many daunting machines and the idea of getting a movement wrong, being mocked or feeling embarrassed is usually enough to deter people from the endeavour of getting fit at all. They'd rather live a less healthy life than be embarrassed trying, or to be seen not getting something right. So why is it that humans fear failure?

If you want to appear really smart you can call this topic 'Atychiphobia' (fear of failure). When looking at this fear of failure that I believe all humans possess to some degree, I think it's important that right off the bat we create a simple means of addressing this early on, and my first bit of advice that has helped me tremendously is to redefine what 'failing' is and what 'failing' looks like.

Let's jump into a scenario I bring up quite frequently in this book, asking someone for their number. I know, a few people by now might be thinking this should have been called *Not A Dating Book* but it's just such a clear and easily understandable situation of fear and inaction intertwined. For so many people, they have defined failing in this situation as being shut down, ignored, given a false number or the person rejecting them, right? Well, a very easy way to redefine failure would be to say, 'If I don't at least try, I'm letting myself down' and seeing that instead as failure. Then as soon as the words 'excuse me …' come out of your mouth you have not failed, you have succeeded irrespective of their response. This is a tactical means of bullet-proofing your realms of success and outcomes from scenarios. Let's look again at an example I use a lot, a job interview. Again, I know many readers will think this book should have been called *Not A Recruitment Book*. But I know so many people are not satisfied with their profession. The Australia Pay Experience Report, released recently by Ceridian found that nearly half of Australian workers (44 per cent) are actively looking for a new job, with another 29 per cent saying that while they're not actively looking, they are open to new opportunities. (See References, p. 263) Also keep in mind that although I use professional life and dating as a means of expression, it does not mean the rules or parameters we outline in this book are exclusive to those two realms alone. This is merely a way of explaining and enabling you to understand. At my business seminars, I often explain marketing as being the same as dating, it helps people understand business processes. If you think about dating, it's marketing. You could call sex the 'business sale' and dating the renewals process. It's a crude means of expressing it, but it often helps people understand principles out of context so they can put them back in. I'm not a rude person, I just like using these tangents to express my points.

I believe it's important that because of statistics like those mentioned before about job dissatisfaction, that we address people's definition of what failing is. If I go for a job interview, perform what I deem to be very well and I don't get the job, is that failing? To many, yes I'd be considered a failure if I didn't get the job. But in reality, it should be redefined. If you put yourself out there, attend a job interview for a job you'd like and you perform well, irrespective of getting the job or not, that's a success. The definition of failing should be that you're not proactively doing anything about your current professional situation. I like to use the analogy of boxing when I talk about success, failure and even making attempts. Not every shot is going to hit your opponent, far from it. But that doesn't and shouldn't ever stop you throwing them. Combinations, reactions to the good, to the bad. Life is like a boxing match, unexpected shots, things get hard, you get cornered and you need to fight your way out of them. Anyone who's ever boxed before will tell you that sometimes you throw a punch without expectations and you land a great connection. Similarly, in sports like football. With shots on target, failing shouldn't be defined as missing the goal. Failing should be defined as not trying to shoot for a goal in the first place. We are the gatekeeper of what we define failure as, just as much as what we define success as, and if we can see failure and define it in a unique way, I honestly believe we can dissipate the fear of failure and instead use any feelings of Atychiphobia to spur us on and motivate us to do something.

You're not a coward to be afraid, you're a coward if you never put yourself in situations where you're not the slightest bit afraid. This chapter isn't about overcoming fear, it's about embracing it and welcoming failure. Get knocked down 7 times and get up 8. We must get comfortable with defining our own metrics of success and we must also define our metrics for failure. We shouldn't be upset when things don't go our way, but instead be happy that we at least made an attempt to improve our situation.

Fear of Being Uncomfortable

There's a type of challenge on the internet called 'The Comfort Zone Challenge' where you ask for a 10 per cent discount on your next cup of coffee. So many people straightaway object to how stupid this is. You don't ask for a discount on most items, unless perhaps at a garage sale or looking to buy a vehicle where there's subjectivity in the cost or value of a thing. But when it comes to ordering a coffee, it's not only an objective cost predetermined by the organisation but not many baristas are in a position to even give the discount. So why is this a challenge? *Because it's not actually about getting a 10 per cent discount.* It's designed to make you look stupid and to get rejected, that's what is going to happen when you ask. You're quite literally facing your fears and the worst possible outcome is going to occur every time you do it. So how is that supposed to benefit you? Rejection, embarrassment and one of the worst things possible: judgement. I can only imagine the barista thinking, 'Who on earth do you think you are?'

I wrote this chapter and shortly after I went for lunch with my business partner, and one thing that haunted me the entire time we ate was that I've written about an example which I could easily do, yet had not done. So without wanting to be a hypocrite I took part in this challenge in the gap between this paragraph and the one before it. I decided there and then I was going to do the challenge. I was hoping there wouldn't be a queue; there wasn't, until I got there of course. I asked for my regular, which is a 'long black with milk please'. This is the Australian way of saying black coffee with a dollop of milk at the top. I've spoken in front of crowds of thousands of people before, yet here I am about to ask for a discount and I'm shitting my pants, I'm breaking down the thoughts in my head and saying to myself, 'Mate, it's just a question.' I then like any normal human being start spinning reasons in my head why not to do it, I even think about deleting the chapter in the book so I can get away with not doing it. I'm doing this in the café within our shared office space, I'm thinking about the consequences of this barista thinking I'm a cheapskate and I'm some kind of piss-taker. Before I know it, there's about four people behind me. I ask for the discount as I'm about to pay. There's a look of confusion on her face, I'm not sure if it's because she thinks I am some kind of self-righteous prick or whether it's because she hasn't heard me. I now have to ask again, but this time loud enough for the other people behind me in the queue. There's a pause and I hear back a 'errr' and I smile. She has already at this point pushed the order to the EFTPOS machine and says to me that she 'doesn't have a discount function on the machine' and that she is sorry. I don't want to seem more pushy, but just as I get my coffee she turns around and grabs something. On her return she gives me a loyalty card I didn't even know existed at this coffee shop, I've had probably a hundred coffees there before. She smiles and says, 'Your tenth coffee is free when you finish the stamp card. That's your 10 per cent off.'

I can't believe something so trivial made me so uncomfortable. The key takeaway was this: in retrospect it was much worse until I had done it, it was never about the tenth coffee being free, it was never about the discount. It was about a tiny little hurdle I could set myself in my path to test myself if I had the minerals to jump it or trip over it. I am so glad I did that, and it could be something you can try in the next 24 hours. Best part is, despite all the fear circling in your mind, your worst-case scenario is that you pay full price for your next coffee. Looking back on the challenge, I realise how fitting the chapter was about the wolves before. Spinning the scenarios in my mind about all the outcomes that could have gone wrong, the embarrassment, the awkwardness or the potential to ruin my favourite coffee shop. There are always more wolves until they're counted. On the other hand, I'm now going to get one in ten coffees for free.

Loss Aversion

Maybe not all fear is just being scared of things or outcomes, perhaps it has something to do with our tendency to naturally feel the psychological pain of losses more than we would the equivalent gains. For instance, losing £10 would feel much worse than the idea of finding £10 on the floor. At one of my recent talks, I used the example of how you can motivate your workforce using loss aversion as a tool. I said that if you hired people who worked on a commission basis, rather than paying them their commission when they hit their target, you can pay them all their commission up front. Should the workers not hit their targets or quotas, you get them to pay you back for all the sales or targets they missed. The psychological pain felt by giving back the money they technically hadn't even earned yet would feel worse, much worse than the idea of not earning it in the first place. You'd probably need a fairly strong legal contract in place, but you get my point.

It's very important to realise that loss aversion doesn't start at zero. What I mean by this is that if, for instance, you were seeking the courage to leave your existing job to pursue a passion and it meant a pay cut from £2,000 a month to £1,600 a month, you'd feel the pain of loss aversion in that pay cut (£400) although still earning £1,600 a month. There was a study done on a group of people where they split a crowd of people into two groups, half of which got given a mug on the way in, the other half got given a chocolate bar on the way in. Now, even if the value of both items was exactly the same, you'd find if offered a swap, a very small amount of people would give up their item, almost like an attachment to it. The idea of losing the mug is more of a pain

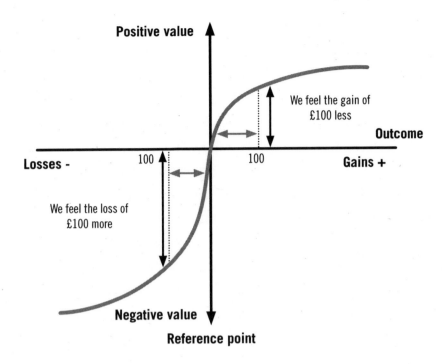

point than the pleasure of gaining the chocolate bar. On the other hand, for the other group of people, the idea of losing the chocolate bar would mean more psychological pain than gaining a mug. Human beings don't like the idea of losing things – this must have an impact on the amount of perceived confidence a human would possess. I always joke around at my talks about this incredible tendency to get attached to things. If I was to ask the mug side of the crowd if they wanted a chocolate bar, no doubt they'd say, 'I can't have a cup of coffee in a chocolate bar, can I?' I'd then turn to the other side (with the chocolate bar) and ask them if they'd like to swap for a mug. I can only imagine someone sat there saying, 'A mug? I can't eat a mug, can I?'

Another example of loss aversion in action is where people let you use a free trial. It's free, you end up making it a part of your life and then when the trial is up you're faced with the idea of losing it, whether it's access to movies, a type of editing tool or a snazzy feature on an app. Loss aversion is utilised to prod your tendency to feel the loss, making you more inclined to avoid the loss by purchasing the product. Another way is that you put things in your 'cart' online. You feel like they're yours before you hit the checkout. Removing items from your cart is a pain point in itself, again making you more likely to buy once you see the bill of all the items put together. So you can understand why people often feel like they lack confidence in the setting of investing, even insurance too. The idea of losing will feel worse than gaining something of the equivalent. If you're thinking of leaving an unsupportive partner, the emotional pain of losing them will feel more than the potential upside of finding someone better suited. Again, financially, when starting your own business or passion project, the idea of your savings being squandered will create more psychological pain than the idea of running your own profitable business where you are the boss.

This emotional connection to losses isn't unique to humans either. Studies have been done on capuchin monkeys where experimenters gave monkeys tokens to trade for food. When they implemented a change in the rules where the monkeys had a 50 per cent win or 50 per cent loss on an item of food, they became a lot more averse to taking chances with the tokens. (See References, p. 263) So keep this in mind whenever you feel like the losses feel like they hold more gravity in a decision-making process and really think about what you want to do and the outcome you desire. If I send you an email saying my sale is about to end, how do you feel? Like you're about to miss out on saving money, right? Again, loss aversion is used every single day everywhere; don't let it take control of your thoughts too much.

So, to close part one, I wanted to really bring your attention to the biases that may be in the way of why we feel we're not confident. Rather than the more common misconception that some people are 'born' confident and some just aren't, confidence is a decision, it's also our relation to failure, not our success. Confidence is a struggle we all face, some of us just deal with our thoughts and outcomes a bit better than others. We all have work to do on our confidence, we're not born confident, it's something we need to build, develop and most importantly keep.

PART II
WHAT NOW?

Chapter 5

Personality Traits and Types

Personality traits reflect people's characteristic patterns of thoughts, feelings and behaviours. It's quite strange in some ways that we're so different, we all like such different things and it's a part of what makes us gel as a society. About a year ago, I was with some friends and we were putting together a big fruit platter for lunch. We got a massive assortment of different fruits and made a big spread for when we came back from an activity we were doing. I said to my friend, 'I wish I liked melons.' He looked at me in such disbelief. 'James, brah, how can you not like melons?!' Then another person chirped their head over and looked at me and said, 'All melons?' I said to them that I just don't like melons, any of them, even watermelons. I wish I did, I really do, they look so delicious and refreshing, but the second I chew on one, my brain says, 'This is disgusting.' My friend said to me that this would be the day when he'd convince me to start eating melon. I said I was open to trying, by all means.

A few hours later when we got back, we began to feast on this fruit platter. I went straight for the pineapple, probably my favourite fruit of all. The same friend said to me he wasn't mad on pineapple. It suddenly dawned on me, and I said to my friends something along the lines of,

'It's actually an incredible thing that our tastes are all so different; if we all sat here with the same likes and dislikes, we'd be left with none of our favourite fruits left and a big pile of all the fruits we dislike; if it wasn't for different tastes, we would not be able to fully enjoy this fruit platter to the full extent it should be.' Now whether or not this revelation came after a big group of us had enjoyed some magic mushrooms or not is irrelevant, the salient idea had come to mind and it's been there to stay since. A uniform approach to likes and dislikes would mean a less enjoyable environment for those eating, let alone the implications to every other area of life.

So when we look at personality traits and the vast differences between us, I think it's a beautiful thing that we're so different, from introversion, extroversion, agreeableness, the lot. We must ensure we appreciate our differences rather than idolising some idea where we're all uniform. It's commonly thought that our personality traits influence which way we lean politically too. I never really paid much attention to politics when I was younger, that's mostly because I thought politics was just about who you elected, not where you stand on current affairs and which way you see things in the world. However, it turns out that personality traits (likes and dislikes, for example) do not cause people to develop political attitudes; rather, there's a correlation between the two, which is a function of an innate common underlying genetic factor in humans. (See References, p. 263)

It's worth noting here that the previous beliefs held by many that your personality was a key driver for your political preference was a prime example of 'correlation does not equal causation'. For instance, as I wrote in *Not A Diet Book*, large red meat consumption is correlated with increased risk of colon cancer. (See References, p. 263) However, it is not the only cause of colon cancer. I know this isn't the same book, but it's a great example of how heuristics can come into play whenever we hear an argument presented. People who typically don't portray many 'health seeking behaviours' will eat more processed foods and therefore more red meats (burgers, sausages, bacon, etc.). People who portray more health seeking behaviours such as getting adequate sleep, stress management, exercise, etc. also usually consume more poultry and fish and consume fewer amounts of foods altogether, therefore consuming less red meat. There is a correlation between red meat and cancer, but it is not a causator. Red meat is not like cigarettes, which are a causator of lung cancer, although many Netflix documentaries with their own agendas would lead you to believe otherwise. (See References, p. 263)

One of the more common online 'personality tests' is the 16Personalities.com test which I've had to do before, when interviewing for a job in the past. I remember first doing it for a role in recruitment nearly a decade ago. I suppose the powers that be wanted to ensure that my personality traits would fit in with my co-workers and peers. Similar to the fruit bowl adage from before, if we were all too similar it could maybe be a disaster. Then again, they say 'opposites attract', but do they work well together? I'm no HR person so I'm not really sure, but when I took the test last time, funnily enough I got a different result than I did today. I have come back today, through writing this book, as a Logician INTP-T. On reflection I think I was a bit more honest with my answers as I knew the importance for this book.

'Logicians often lose themselves in thought – which isn't necessarily a bad thing. People with this personality type hardly ever stop thinking. From the moment they wake up, their minds buzz with ideas, questions, and insights. At times, they may even find themselves conducting fully-fledged debates in their own heads.' (See References, p. 263)

What I want to draw your attention to next is this: there is no personality type that comes out as 'Confident'. The 16 personality types are: Architect, Logician, Commander, Debater, Advocate, Mediator, Protagonist, Campaigner, Logistician, Defender, Executive, Consul, Virtuoso, Adventurer, Entrepreneur and Entertainer. So hold on a minute, where is the confidence personality type? Are they mistaken? Have they missed the 17th personality type? The answer is no.

'There is a widely held perception (or misperception), that confidence directly correlates to Introversion and Extraversion. More specifically, Extraverts are highly confident and Introverts lack confidence. At first glance, the data seems to show that the assumption holds true; however, there are famous examples of highly successful Introverts, like Mark Zuckerberg, who exude quiet and highly genuine confidence. Obviously, there are more personality traits involved in the influence of confidence.'

In a bid to better understand the link between personality type and confidence, the smart cookies at 16Personalities.com asked their community to agree or disagree with the statement 'you have genuine confidence in your abilities'. They spread the answers across all

16 personality types and they uncovered the trait among all the personality types with the strongest influence on people's sense of genuine confidence: identity.

So again, remember that your personality is not what determines your confidence or your self-esteem, it just portrays what your personality is. As mentioned earlier in the book, confidence plays a tremendous part in your relationship to failure, and the fact that so many people go through life wanting to avoid failure by any means possible.

NACH versus NAF

Bringing me right back to my BTEC in Sports Performance and Excellence back in college, we learned about NACH and NAF personality traits. Achievement Motivation is a well-studied field and sports psychologists have tried to determine for years why some performers are just happy to take part while others play to win. Athletes (and people in general, as I'll get on to later in the chapter) either face a challenge head-on or avoid it all together.

Let's say you're squatting at your local CrossFit gym: the first workout is about seeing who can squat the most in comparison to their weight over three sets. Some people on their last set will increase the weight to a point they may fail, but they want to get the best score in the gym. Others will keep the weight at a 'safe' amount to avoid them failing or not completing the rep. Here's an example of the difference between NACH and NAF.

NACH = Need to Achieve

NAF = Need to Avoid Failure

Whoever went for the added amount of weight would be the person with their sights set on the need to achieve, whereas the other playing it safe is more motivated by avoiding failure. Another example of this would be the kicker in a game of rugby: what motivates him, the need to hit the kick and score? Or the worries of missing and telling his captain it's better to kick 'for touch' instead? An example of seeing both in unison would be a classic tennis serve: the first serve in most cases is a NACH for an ace, however with a change in circumstances on the second serve, it's a case of NAF and better to avoid failure so you don't give up easy points.

Many of our decisions in life are based around these principles if you think about it. 'Playing it safe' is a part of the mindset of NAF, of needing to avoid failure. Not asking for a promotion or pay rise, not asking for a number or not asking someone out, not starting a business or not going for it, is part of a well-studied personality trait of people motivated by avoiding failure. Those with a hunger to achieve, who do not care about the losses, the misses, but instead are fuelled by a need for winning, of achieving, are those who add the weight to the bar, opt for the posts and set their sights only on what 'winning' is to them.

> 'I've missed more than 9,000 shots in my career. I've lost almost 300 games; 26 times I've been trusted to take the game-winning shot and missed. I've failed over and over and over again in my life. And that is why I succeed.'
>
> Michael Jordan

Anyone who watched the documentary *The Last Dance* on Netflix will see how fiercely competitive Michael Jordan is, with gambling, bets and basketball. His desire to achieve is inspiring and in my opinion, infectious to the people who he played alongside.

I don't believe we are fixed in our ways, we're malleable and we're able to change who we are and how we act. I think even just understanding our actions, we can now look at parts of our life and see where we're NACH and where we're NAF. I don't think it's a bad trait to want to avoid failure, but I think it's better we look to set our sights on achieving, and that we ask ourselves, what could we accomplish if we set our sights more on a need to achieve in certain situations rather than constantly looking to do anything to avoid failing at something? A lesson we can learn from Michael Jordan is, if you're willing to fail enough, you can then possess what is necessary to become truly successful. He never for a moment was truly worried about losing, his sights were set too tightly on winning.

Internal versus External Confidence

Let's break up confidence into two segments:

- ▶ Internal confidence, which could be how we think, what we believe, how we rate our abilities for instance, just to mention a few.
- ▶ External confidence, which could be how we dress, how we stand and move, how we sit and how we speak, to name a few.

Internal thoughts and feelings are very important on a daily basis to reign in and check in on – a very popular method of meditation is known as 'ascension' and it focuses on this. Some people I hold in very high regard use this as a means of moving the mind towards thinking about praise, gratitude and compassion to themselves. Yes, people literally sit there saying nice stuff to themselves to feel better. But I think a large part of this is down to **who we think we are**. Yes, that's right, **who we think we are**. If I was to get you to write down who you are, you may say you're 'shy' which could be correct, but soon it becomes a part of the story you tell yourself about who you are. The danger of listening to the story we tell ourselves is that sometimes it can be to our detriment. Ryan Holiday wrote a fantastic book called *Ego is the Enemy* which really got me thinking about the story I tell myself about my life and especially any success I've experienced. When auditing my story, by thinking about it in great depth I came to realise we can often glamourise elements such as thinking, 'I was smart enough to do (insert what you did).' But in reality, listening to my story easily causes me to overlook the days that were a struggle, the early morning alarms and the days I slogged a 12-hour day on 5 hours of sleep and 7 coffees. We can overhype the times we got lucky and we all too easily overlook the times we truly grafted. So the story we tell ourselves is of vital importance because it plays a big role in who we are on a daily basis. If you say you're a shy person, you'll act that way because you're living the beliefs of your identity. If you can stop labelling yourself as shy, it's a first internal step to becoming a version of yourself that's more outgoing.

Internal belief is of great importance because it is going to impact the amount of action that you will take. Remember earlier on I spoke about a martial artist teaching a kid to punch through a block of wood. Often, they don't strike it hard enough because they don't think it will break, the instructor would then say 'you can do this' and sure enough the belief changes, then voilà, a kid somewhere just punched through a block of wood. (Disclaimer: I don't know where you'd go to get these blocks of wood. 'Hey, do you sell punching blocks of wood here?') Anyway let's not get distracted, you get the deal. If you don't believe you can accomplish something, you won't possess the right mindset to properly action it. Internal belief in what you can or can't do has such a big part to play in how things will turn out. It's not easy convincing ourselves we're capable of things, it takes repetition and often proving to ourselves that we are.

> 'The confidence people have in their beliefs is not a measure of the quality of evidence but of the coherence of the story the mind has managed to construct.'
>
> Daniel Kahneman

There are 4 key areas to consider when we think about internal confidence:

- **Thoughts:** our thoughts are not automated, they're processes that we control each and every moment of each day. We must override them when they don't serve us, when we doubt and put ourselves down.
- **Image:** how we see ourselves, because we have tendencies to have a distorted image in our minds of how we look. Body dysmorphia, I think, exists in every single human being; some

people suffer worse than others but it's important we hone-in on what we like about ourselves. It's all too easy to get lost in areas of our bodies we don't like.

▶ **Growth:** there are always days that everything seems impossible and like it's an uphill battle. Reflecting on your growth, your journey and how far you've managed to make it so far can dampen any thoughts of doubt and struggle.

▶ **Values:** when trying to muster internal confidence we must lean and rely on our values of what is important to us. When making decisions we must lean into what suits our values, not what suits other people. If you're making a decision based on your values, you should have the confidence to do it based on that alone.

External confidence is how we dress, how we hold ourselves and even the tone of voice we use. Our external presentation of our confidence is such an interesting topic. There's a lot of trails of thought surrounding how we feel that make us act a certain way, but also that how we act can change how we feel. People analyse so many things without even knowing, like how wide your feet are as you stand, how you sit too. Outside any job interview you'll see people portraying very anxious sitting patterns, folded forward, elbows on knees, making themselves very small. Before interviewing in corporate jobs back in the day, I made it a point of sitting back with my arm around the back of the chair next to me. The way I saw it, if I couldn't feel confident at least I could pretend I felt confident when it came to the interview room, but there may be some truth to this actually working.

In Daniel Kahneman's brilliant book *Thinking, Fast and Slow* his experimenters did an experiment getting students to watch a cartoon at the same time as holding a pencil in their mouths in one of two different ways: one group had the pencil in sideways so they had to force a smile to watch, the other group had it in pointing away from them, which forced them to frown. The students with the pencil in sideways rated the cartoons as being much funnier. This would bolster the argument that actions can precede emotions. You may think these things wouldn't make that much of a difference, but they do.

If you don't believe me, type 'Rolex' into Google images and you'll notice all the clocks are set to 10.10 a.m. (sometimes also 1.50 p.m.) so that the hands resemble a smile. There are aesthetic benefits too: for instance the hands are symmetrical which human eyes like to see. The hands almost frame the watchmaker's logo, but the main reason is, yes, to make the watch look like it's smiling, therefore more likeable and more likely that you'd buy it. Every day is a school day, right? These small but subtle differences are everywhere, from people smiling in adverts on TV to prearranged clock hands on watches to improve the buyer experience. The smallest changes can have a big impact on our perceptions. I'm not saying that this is enough in itself to reverse emotions, I wouldn't ever think for a second to say to someone experiencing malaise or sadness to just put a pencil in their mouth sideways in a bid to cheer up. However, it's interesting to see the results of experiments on what impact small changes to our bodies can have on our minds.

Non-verbal Confidence AKA 'Body Language'

Imagine I create a test where someone walks into a room, sits down and says nothing for a minute. Do you think you'd be able to gauge with any kind of accuracy how confident that person is?

Think about the last few times you've said to someone 'are you okay?' or 'are you alright?' These often present themselves after recognising certain non-verbal behaviours in people.

If you scour the internet, you'll find different claims and articles that only 7 per cent of our communication is verbal. If only 7 per cent is what we say, then how we say it is a huge factor that cannot be overlooked, right? There are also good videos online where people can make the same sentence have multiple meanings; marketing coaches use this to explain to their audiences how important the emphasis on a certain word is for the right outcome. The technical word for this is 'intonation'. Intonation is variation in pitch used to indicate the speaker's attitudes and emotions, to highlight or focus an expression. (See References, p. 263) I know this is a bit of a tangent but I do want to arm you with the importance of changes to verbal communication before moving into non-verbal communication.

One of my favourite examples on intonation is one I saw online a while back. If you were to really emphasise on the highlighted text, it gives the same words a new meaning:

I didn't say we should kill him. = Someone else said we should kill him.

I **didn't** say we should kill him. = I am denying saying it.

I didn't **say** we should kill him. = I implied it/whispered it/wrote it
down.

I didn't say **we** should kill him. = I said someone else should kill
him/you should kill him, etc.

I didn't say we **should** kill him. = I said we shouldn't kill him/we
must kill him, etc.

I didn't say we should **kill** him. = I said we should take him to
dinner/take care of him/send him on a diving holiday.

I didn't say we should kill **him**. = We should kill someone else.

There are many nuances to how verbal communication is pronounced to make an impact on the listener. So I don't think 7 per cent is a very accurate means of quantifying the verbal component of communication. Actually, in fact, while researching for this book I found that the commonly known and recited 7 per cent verbal and 93 per cent non-verbal communication statistic is widely disputed. A journalist named Philip Yaffe debunked the original studies and said, 'Because the figures were so easy to remember, most people forgot about what they really meant. Hence, the myth that communication is only 7 per cent verbal and 93 per cent non-verbal was born. And we have been suffering from it ever since.'

There is no easy to remember adage when it comes to the split of communication between verbal and non-verbal, a bit like the saying 'it's 80 per cent diet and 20 per cent training'. There is too much nuance in these and many subjects to label them as a dichotomy. Body language is a huge thing, and it's even well studied down to the fact that using hand gestures and gesticulating can help people understand the tone of what you're saying and better receive what you say. (See References,

p. 263) 'It's not what you say, it's how you say it.' (See References, p. 263) Which isn't just a truth, it's a common accusation often heard in any argument between couples. This is why I opt to use a headset microphone for speaking engagements too, if you've ever wondered, that is. I know comics like to use a microphone as part of their act; they can use the wire and it's arrangement to kill a bit of time between bits. Not only that, but wired microphones often have less feedback, so comics and comedians can really change the pitch and tone of their voice, even screaming into the microphone without feedback from the audio system. But myself, I much prefer using a headset because it allows me to use my arms to explain my points in a way that not only feels cognitively easier, it allows me to communicate with more than just my words and just my punctuation. This is why it's common to see TED speakers using a headset too: this not only frees up the hands to gesture, but also to use devices such as clickers for presentations, which is another thing I'd advise for any of you that are going to dabble into the realm of public speaking. When you move your hands to explain what you are talking about, you will help your audience understand your points. A study by the University of Chicago showed that what a speaker does with their hands as they gesture facilitates understanding by the audience members. (See References, p. 263) The study concluded that if you don't use your hands, your audience will judge you as a less charismatic leader, and they will not understand as much of your presentation.

There are so many cues that people pick up on, but it's important that the combination of verbal and non-verbal communication isn't really split into a dichotomy and instead seen as a whole presentation style that can be benefited from using your hands in a sincere and genuine way to back up your points.

Fake it 'Til You Make it, Right?

'Fake it 'til you make it' is a terminology that's been thrown around loosely for years. The saying first appeared around 1973, and the earliest reference to a very similar saying occurs in the Simon & Garfunkel song 'Fakin' It'. In that song Simon sings, 'And I know I'm fakin' it, I'm not really makin' it.' (See References, p. 263) However, I think the terminology is much more widely known from the TED speaker Amy Cuddy. I remember watching this as long ago as nearly seven or eight years. This TED talk which is hosted on YouTube had a whopping 39 million views by 2017 alone. (See References, p. 263) Amy Cuddy is a social psychologist and if you watch the video you're left thinking, 'Wow, I just need to stand differently, and I can unlock my full potential.'

I've always been slightly sceptical of anything purported in a TED talk, because of **commercial interest**. I'll quickly inform you what a 'TED talk' is just in case you've not heard of one before. A TED talk is a showcase for speakers presenting great, well-formed ideas in under 18 minutes. (See References, p. 263) The 'well-formed' idea can be one of two things:

- ► Something that's new and surprising; an idea or invention that your audience has never heard about.
- ► A great basic idea (that your audience has maybe already heard) with a compelling new argument behind it that challenges beliefs and perspectives.

However, their content guidelines strictly prohibit commercial agendas, political agendas, inflammatory rhetoric, religious agendas, and bad science.

I completed my first TED talk in 2019 in Bundaberg, Australia. You have quite literally 18 minutes to complete the talk. (They tell you just before you step on stage 'no longer than 18 minutes or it won't get uploaded to YouTube.') This makes you a bit nervous because, well, for a start speaking at such an event is a big deal, you're considered to have something compelling to speak about, you don't want to mess this up. But the second is that at the time of speaking, TED had over 20 million subscribers. So it's quite literally your time in the limelight.

You're given the reins, the opportunity to quite literally say what you want to, and should this resonate or have even the slightest element of virality the commercial interest is vast, unimaginable. This is why I sometimes always take TED talks with a pinch of salt. (Fun fact: 'pinch of salt' originated sometime in the Middle Ages and always simply referred to making dull food more exciting, or a tall tale easier to swallow, by sprinkling a bit of salt on it.) (See References, p. 263)

Anyway, not to get distracted with interesting facts that you can take to your next pub quiz. We can all too often see the temptation when presenting personal stories with a pinch of ideology and subjectivity. For instance, referring back to the Amy Cuddy 'Your body language may shape who you are' video, there were many disputes right off the bat, especially within the realm of 'hormone testing' that was involved in the studies mentioned in her talk. Initially, Amy says that you need to go into a toilet cubicle, close the door and raise your arms above your head to raise your testosterone and lower your cortisol. There is a lot of dispute about these sorts of claims, which seem to me to be using scarce evidence to back up previously held stand-points. For instance, when disputing some of the methods used in this talk: salivary testosterone testing is influenced by sample collection, leakage of blood from the gums, storage conditions and gender differences to name a few, making it a very inaccurate means of testing someone's true testosterone, let alone whether it's influenced by posture and body language in such a short period of time. (See References, p. 263)

I'm not doubting or rejecting what's said in all TED talks; I admire and have been inspired by so many. Just to say they're not studies, they're not necessarily gospel. Some are very ideological and some are merely ideas, not evidence. I think it should be of utmost importance to be realistic with this means and method of inspiring people's confidence around the world.

Here's a question to consider within the context of Amy Cuddy's talk: can you become more hireable with a certain type of body language? The answer appears to be yes. (See References, p. 263) Participants in a study adopted one of two types of pose: high-power (i.e. expansive, open) or low-power (i.e. contractive, closed). Now although there are holes to pick in sending someone into a toilet cubicle to alter their hormonal state, I do tend to agree with Amy Cuddy's claims about posture in winners and losers. If I Google image search 'winning poses' or even ask you to think about it – the arms in the air, wide open chest, broad posture – it's holding your medal in the air for everyone to see it. Even the most introverted person in a moment of winning will enlarge their being to the widest possible. In the much watched TED talk, Amy Cuddy even expressed that blind people who have never witnessed seeing someone celebrate also by nature adopt the expansive stance when they win. Insinuating that winning posture is something shared across all cultures and is something that's quite humanely shared. A bit like when someone is shocked; it doesn't matter if you're in China, Uganda or Wales, you'd pull the same expression when you were deeply surprised by something. The contractive and closed posture we all know well. Whether it's being in a hospital waiting room, being nervous, outside a job interview or slightly intimidated in an unfamiliar area or territory, we naturally make ourselves small. We all try to snap out of it, we catch ourselves the moment our forearms hit our knees and we convince ourselves to sit back; we say to ourselves when we're uncomfortable in new environments in our mind, 'Don't appear to be nervous.'

I'm sure many readers of this book have done the exact thing when you arrive on a date as the first person. You sit down at the table, get your phone out and message the other person. 'I'm here, no rush.' Then you catch yourself hunched over, small and insecurely sat. You sit back and try to portray a much more confident stance, you then notice the sweat in your palms on the table. You then wipe your hands on your leg every 30 seconds knowing your date could walk in at any second. You want to ensure your palm is cool and not clammy, so you can seem cool. It's hard work to pretend you're not shitting yourself, yet we all do it as hard as we can. I mentioned in my last book, always ask for a glass of water when interviewing. Take a sip just before a question is asked to give yourself an extra second to think of the answer; also hold the glass in your right hand when moving around the office, as this will cool it down ready for any handshakes that come out of left field. (Fun fact: 'out of left field' is American slang meaning 'unexpected'. Really, every day is a school day in this book.)

Back to the study I was talking about before, participants had to prepare a speech for a mock interview. They were videotaped for overall performance and hireability, *those who prepared for the job interview with high- (vs. low-) power poses performed better and were more likely to be chosen for hire; this relation was mediated by nonverbal presence, but not by verbal content.* (See References, p. 263) This goes to show that how you say things can certainly influence the outcome of the situation, even if it doesn't alter your hormonal state.

We need to put an end to this incessant need to stop our hormonal state; I'm sure the 'expectation effect' plays a role in how we feel. I mean, if we go into a toilet cubicle and raise our hands in the air, I'm sure if we expect it's going to make us feel more confident it probably will work in some respect. But hormones aren't going to be the best place to search for metrics of success, are they?

Who really is checking their hormones several times a day? This is why I have such issues with people claiming they're experts in 'biohacking'. There are people online who say they're going to change your hormones, but no one is exactly getting their iPhone out to check their cortisol levels to determine how that cold shower benefited their stress levels, are they? Instead, we need to take note of how we feel about something, then probe into why we feel that way, see if the thought is warranted or even valid in the first place. Should we determine that the feeling of anxiety, worry or fear of failure isn't warranted, we begin putting into place an internal justification of why we should prepare ourselves as much as we can, then own the situation to the best of our ability and hold ourselves not as someone we're not, but someone deserving of where we are. If you look at a job interview for instance, you wouldn't be invited to the office or on a Zoom call if you

143

weren't a valid candidate for the role. If you're given the time of day, it's very unlikely that you're merely cannon fodder. Every other applicant for the role is just as nervous as you, they hold the same thoughts of worry and fear of failing. This is not a time to think about anything other than to hold yourself as the person you are, someone capable and competent to go after what you desire. This isn't about being someone else, it's about being yourself fully.

I love a story that a comedian called Chris DiStefano told about the time he was extremely nervous going on David Letterman's *The Late Show* back in 2013. None other than John Travolta was in the green room backstage with him. Just before the comedian stepped on stage, John put his hand rather uncomfortably on Chris's chest and said, 'The work is done.' He reminded Chris that there was no reason to be nervous, he had done everything necessary to be in that green room. He told him that now it was time to enjoy the result of the hard work, to go out and just enjoy it. I love the idea that when we find ourselves in very uncomfortable situations, much of the work has already been done, so there isn't as much to be as nervous about. If you've got a big pitch or presentation, chances are the work has been done months and years beforehand. When it's time to perform, as much as there is the requirement to do well, it's not the time to worry. The work has been done, just enjoy it the most you can. You wouldn't be there if you weren't capable of doing it. Being confident isn't about becoming someone new, it's about becoming the person you can and often rightfully should be. Your ancestors fought off famine and predators in the wild for thousands of years on end, trust me when I say you have what it takes to hold yourself well, present and speak clearly and not just say what you need to, but to say it exactly how you should.

Can we fake it until we make it? To me, no. Why? Because we shouldn't be faking who we are. We don't for a second want to live within a fake identity. For a start it will clash with a lot of people's values, especially those people who want to be genuine. Authenticity is something you should aspire to at all times, unapologetically. It may not make you the most liked in the room, but it will set you up for being happier long term. I've faked it before, worn suits and pretended to be of the corporate cloth, but to be honest it felt more like suffocating than it did a viable means of progressing in life. Being an imposter is an unavoidable position you'll find yourself in during your lifetime, but being authentic is optional and I fully suggest you don't trade authenticity for anything life can offer you. One of my biggest issues with the 'fake it 'til you make it' ideal is that to do this properly requires you to ignore your feelings and emotions. Having a finger on the pulse of your emotions to me is an essential part of dealing with and overcoming them. To pretend they don't exist doesn't sit well with me as a recipe for success.

Our feelings aren't always correct, but they're there for a reason: to tell us something, to play a part where thoughts and physiology collide. They should be dealt with, sure, but not ignored. It's completely normal to feel like you don't belong somewhere, it's completely normal to feel like you don't know what you're doing. I think there's strength in accepting that, and given the choice of pretending to be great at something versus the humility to accept you need some support and help from your peers, colleagues or friends, authenticity will and should always come out on top.

What is 'making it'? We are all curators of our own visions of what success looks like. What are we epitomising here? Is 'making it' pretending to be something you're not, in a higher position? Is that what we're deeming as success? Why can't 'making it' be unapologetic authenticity? Personally, I could be a lot more popular worldwide and have amassed much higher earnings by faking it, by being a people pleaser and toning down my constant swearing. But for me that's a bad deal, more money isn't 'making it' to me. Almost paradoxically, authenticity and being genuine is my means of success. Pretending to be someone I'm not, may mean more money, but I'd lose happiness as a by-product of that decision.

Imagine you're in a boardroom and someone has been appointed as leader for a task at hand. What do you think you'd prefer from that person, to pretend they know it all or to admit they're perhaps insecure with being in that role? There is huge power in vulnerability – it creates trust in relationships, both professionally and personally, and allows people to learn from one another and therefore enhance their authentic strengths. While I can't help but feel that pretending to be something you're not only magnifies the void in your own levels of confidence. Whereas being yourself and authentic from the get-go can only improve the levels of confidence you have within. Feel like an imposter? Anyone in that position would. I can't help but think that you have two types of people: those who feel like an imposter in their own lives and those who are pretending as hard as they can that they're not. The latter will eventually have to break character, the façade can only last so long.

Want to know a real superpower in life? Being yourself. We don't have enough time on this spinning planet floating through an ever-expanding void of nothingness to go on dates pretending to be someone we're not. Life's too short to pretend you're a different person to who you really are. You may have less friends and acquaintances but being yourself is the easiest way in life to make it, without ever having to fake it.

Chapter 6

Choosing Life's Passengers

Say you're going on a really long trip in the car, doesn't sound so bad, does it? You could put on a nice long podcast, or audiobook. But what if I said you had to have a passenger? Suddenly that trip is either going to go two ways, amazing or terrible. The differentiator here is going to be who comes with you and who doesn't. I want to apply this same thought process to life in general. There are people who are passengers in your life who are going to be giving you compliments, others who gee you up to push your boundaries, to take risks and to support you if things go wrong, which they can. Then there are the unsupportive passengers, those who through whatever reasons doubt your abilities and at times even gaslight you. I'm not sure the root of this, if I am honest, sometimes I think people care about you so much they want to see you safe, so safe that inadvertently they don't want to see you succeed. Unfortunately, I think a large number of people don't truly want you to win because it will make them feel bad about themselves. When looking to make the positive changes to your life that I hope you will from this book, it's important that you note not everyone will be able to come on this journey with you. Those who you surround yourself with are either the wind in your sails or the headwind you're up against in your journey of life.

Quick revisit: If you read either of my other books, you'll remember the sunk cost fallacy: don't cling onto a mistake because you were a long time making it. Just because you've been with someone for years, it doesn't mean they are **right**. Human beings tend to find it harder to walk away from something depending on the previous amount of energy, time and money spent on it. It's called the sunk cost *because the cost is already lost*. You need to make decisions based on what's right, not what is going to prevent previous resources going to waste.

Inspired Confidence

What is inspiration? According to the dictionary, it's 'the process of being mentally stimulated to do or feel something, especially to do something creative'. Whether we know it or not, we are inspired by those around us to do things. American entrepreneur Jim Rohn once famously said, 'You are the average of the 5 people you spend the most time with.'

I think it's really important that we truly understand this. Our peers, friends and colleagues will inspire us whether we know it or not. We will also become inspired by those we follow, or subscribe to. For instance, I very much hope that by reading this book or alternatively listening to several hours of me speaking, that I elicit a response in your brain to become mentally stimulated to do something, I wish to inspire you. So what is it that gives us the inspiration to try things? Well, I expect it has a lot to do with the fact we can see it has been done. Joe Rogan has the largest podcast in the world, it started off very small and for years even he will admit not many people even listened to it. It's the

148

biggest in the world because he was not only an early adapter to podcasts, but he remained very consistent in the years after beginning. So many people, perhaps without realising it, are no doubt inspired by this story and much more inclined to start a podcast of their own. I'll admit, starting a podcast is incredibly daunting, my fear of creating one meant I chose to hide behind a guise of saying, 'I'm too good looking to have a podcast.' The truth was I wasn't yet inspired enough to take action. What it eventually took was for me to see it working for other people around me, and before long I had enough inspiration to be 'courageous' enough to begin. Now hundreds of episodes in, I am what I would call a fairly decent podcaster. At the time of writing this book, there's over 2 million podcasts available worldwide, whereas in 2018 there were just over half a million. (See References, p. 263) You can see this trend is on a massive upward trajectory. So why are so many people participating in such a trend? I believe that they've been inspired to do something out of their comfort zone.

It's not enough to know the juice is worth the squeeze. We still need to find inspiration in knowing we can accomplish something. There are so many things that are outside our comfort zone that we could do each day to better our position. Inspiration is almost the magic emotion we require to step into the daunting and uncomfortable experience to reap the reward. I've often said to people who 'need motivation' that perhaps they don't think the work is worth it. If I said to you, do 100 burpees and I'll give you £1,000, you'd probably do it – you know the work is worth it. With many things in life, we're not sure if the work is worth it, but when we're inspired by seeing someone else do it, it ignites a necessary switch in our brains to want to pursue it.

This exists in so many contexts. Seeing a friend taking a break from their work life to go travel the world. Seeing a colleague quit their job to start their own business. A friend approaches a stranger to successfully get their number. It's important that we decide to seek inspiration from these moments when we see them. All too often people can look at other people's success through the wrong lens and become bitter. Tall poppy syndrome is a societal attitude that occurs when people are resented, disliked or criticised due to their successes. (See References, p. 263) To keep a row of poppies uniform, if one was to stick up above the rest you'd cut it down instead of praising its growth. So many people unfortunately see other people's success like this, instead of looking at it as a means of inspiring themselves to reach a higher level. I'm going to talk about progressive overload a little later in this book (see page 226), but for now I just want you to understand that it's important that those you seek inspiration from also leave your mind, your passions and objectives in a position of being stretched. Confucius famously said, 'If you are the smartest in the room, you're in the wrong room.' I tend to agree, should there be no one surrounding you that inspires you, you may not be in the right place. It doesn't have to be a physical room either. But I like to keep well connected to those that inspire me, that excel in their own fields, so I can draw inspiration to edge closer to them instead of resenting their position for being better than I currently am. Being inspired by the right people keeps you humble. If I just sit back and look at what I've accomplished, no doubt I'll begin to think, 'Wow, I'm getting really good at this now.' But the power of being inspired by someone doing better than you at a higher standard keeps you honest.

Confidence and inspiration exist within a paradigm that prevents you from stumbling across arrogance or being too cocky. Joe Rogan makes me into a better podcaster, yet it keeps me from thinking I'm too good because I am all too aware of how much more work I'd need to do to get close to his level. I'm quite literally over 10,000 hours behind him. The amount of time it takes to come close to mastery, he's already ahead. Being more creative with content, I'll seek inspiration from those funnier than me, more engaging than me and who plan their content better. I'm not copying them either, that's the important thing to explain. Being inspired is not plagiarising someone's work and pretending it's your own. It's seeing success in something and inspiring confidence in yourself to create similar success of your own. All knowledge comes from those who came before us.

> *'If I have seen further, it is by standing upon the shoulders of giants.'*
>
> Sir Isaac Newton

It's very important we realise none of us can ever truly be unique or original with what we do because we're inspired by someone before; even Joe Rogan was inspired by Adam Curry's podcast which aired before Joe's. The 'Joe Rogan Experience' also was inspired by 'The Jimmy Hendrix' Experience. This doesn't discredit Rogan's incredible journey, it just shows that he stood on the shoulders of giants before him.

I can't write this chapter without talking about jiu-jitsu, but I want to draw attention to the fact that success leaves clues. At the time of writing this book, the pound for pound most successful no-gi grappler is Gordan Ryan. It's no secret that he developed his skills from John

Danaher who is arguably one of the most knowledgeable coaches of all time in martial arts. He spent his career in Renzo Gracie's gym in New York, getting his black belt from a member of the Gracie family who are notable for the creation of the world's fastest growing martial art, jiu-jitsu. Social media platforms like TikTok are revolutionising the social media scene through allowing creators to be inspired by other people's creations and using the same sounds and features to create content. It's imperative that we see the world as not those who are creative and those who are not, but instead as people who take inspiration from others' success and use that success as leverage to muster confidence within themselves to go after something, not to see success as a reason to become bitter. I feel sorry for people who I'd call 'haters', all that energy and effort wasted on disliking someone when you could all too easily seek inspiration from the same person and do better because of it.

To conclude, never underestimate the importance of exposing yourself to others' success where you can be inspired by their actions to create confidence in yourself. If you only expose yourself to people who aren't accomplishing, it may portray a reality where you're likely to fail if you put yourself out there to try. However, if you engage in whatever medium you like, whether podcasts, books, talks or even YouTube with people who truly inspire you, you'll feel a tremendous amount more confident in what you take on next.

Passing Inspiration Forward

This is where things get really interesting. Let's say you draw inspiration from the right people, leverage their experiences to build confidence in yourself and you experience some form of success, irrespective of the level or heights of that success. Without realising it you're going to inspire those people around you, who will then draw inspiration from your success. This is a gift that keeps on giving: the value goes far and beyond your own successful experiences, it then impacts the people around you. I'm a big believer in the fact that the path you carve out for yourself in life can be for whoever you wish to follow you on it.

Confidence is infectious, it really is. If I go back to my days working within sales departments for various businesses, it was my job to cold call people all day and try to find opportunities within businesses to sell the product I was assigned to. This wasn't very sexy stuff, I can assure you. 'Hello, James Smith here, I'm calling to try to determine what needs your business may have to log management software?' Riveting, right? So what did every sales department do? Bunched us together, really close, with a leader among the team to whip us all into action. Confidence in a group setting requires leadership encapsulating my two previous points, the combination of confidence and inspiration. A leader must inspire confidence into their group. Sales teams have done this for as long as I could remember with tales of crazy incentives. 'Steve from the (insert big firm here) account closed a bonus last quarter of £21,000 and bought himself a BMW!' This is the leader inspiring us with someone else's success to make it seem more accomplishable. Similar to the previous chapter (see page 43) when

Tim Ferriss inspired the students to contact someone famous. Without the inspiration to be courageous, they would not muster the confidence to take appropriate action. Any start-up business requires a trifecta of those three things: leadership, inspiration and confidence.

Destructive Inspiration – Gaslighting

Women can call the Freephone National Domestic Abuse Helpline run by Refuge on 0808 2000 247 at any time, day or night. The staff will offer confidential, non-judgemental information and support.

Gaslighting is the killer of inspiration, therefore in my eyes a silent saboteur to confidence.

Gaslighting is a form of manipulation that often occurs most commonly in abusive relationships. It is a covert type of emotional abuse where the bully or abuser misleads the target, creating a false narrative and making them question their judgements and reality. (See References, p. 263)

> *'Confidence is contagious. So is lack of confidence.'*
>
> Vince Lombardi

Gaslighting is one of those things that you didn't quite realise existed until you're either a victim of it, or someone truly explains where it's happening and you recognise it. Gaslighting is a form of verbal manipulation where someone can control you by slowly making you doubt yourself over and over which will erode any self-sense of confidence.

One of the most interesting methods gaslighters will use when they lie is repetition of a lie. Neil deGrasse Tyson, the American astrophysicist, famously said that there are three different truths in the world: objective truths (these are proven by evidence), personal truths (from beliefs like religion, so not objective, but it's true to you), and political truths (which are true through incessant repetition). 'Repeat a lie often enough and it becomes the truth', is a law of propaganda often attributed to the Nazi Joseph Goebbels. It's also a studied field where people tend to rate things they've seen, heard or read before, as more likely to be true. (See References, p. 263)

Repetition in this field is not to be taken for granted, so imagine someone repeatedly saying to you 'you're an idiot' or 'you can't be trusted with important tasks'. When you question someone or push back on these comments, you may even get responses such as 'you're so dramatic' or 'you're being dramatic again'. Although these may not be true, if repeated enough you may believe they are. When looking at the emotions associated with gaslighting you'll find confusion, thinking something is wrong with you, doubting your feelings, doubting your reality, feeling powerless and many more emotions that are counterproductive to achieving a sense or feeling of confidence.

The reason I include gaslighting in this book about confidence is not only because it plays a big role in diminishing so many people's self-esteem and confidence, but because the way it impacts another really important aspect to developing confidence, our inner narrative.

The Inner Narrative

Our inner narrative is what we tell ourselves each day; it's our inner monologue to how we see and perceive the world. It's how we collate our experiences to make a story out of our life. Everyone has a slightly different narrative, because everyone has a combination of different events and experiences. Our inner narrative, our inner monologue, is what you could even call 'self-talk'. When processing cognitive or emotional thoughts, we rely on this inner narrative. Interrogative self-talk (which I will talk about on page 231), is the way we challenge ourselves inside our own heads. Our inner voice isn't just there to think through problems though, we all have a unique way of how we see ourselves and how we perceive our place in the world. Our thoughts and our realities combine to figure out why the world is what we think it is. I'll remember something last minute and my inner narrative will say, 'I have such a good memory.' This is short lived, because it will only be half an hour later and I've gone somewhere without my AirPods. I'll share with you an example of this I've experienced a lot in the last few years. I have over the last few years attempted to create the most engaging and sometimes viral social media content; this has accrued quite literally tens of millions of views. This never happened before I was 28 years old, so I have nearly three decades of experience of people **not** recognising me. You'd not believe the places I've had someone come speak to me, in the furthest corners of an airport in Singapore, on the dancefloor at Coachella, all the way to being on the beach in Australia or out for dinner with my parents in the UK. Sometimes, someone will lock eyes with me and it's not in the normal way they would; I can sense and feel their cognitive processes from across the room, I can very frequently see them accessing their temporal lobe to remember where they know me from. (See References, p. 263) Don't worry, I didn't know which part of the brain did that before writing this book, every day's a school day, right? So there I am locking eyes with someone for a split second as their gaze exists for just that half a second too long and 'bam!', my inner narrative kicks in to put some sense in my head. 'James, don't be a narcissistic prick, they're just looking at you, they don't recognise you.' I smile to myself and then a bit more abuse to keep me humble occurs. 'Your videos aren't that amazing mate, you're not that well-known and that person is probably just trying to figure out why your haircut is so off trend or why you're wearing flip flops during winter.' Then two minutes later, 'You're that guy from Facebook, you've come up in my feed for years.' I smile and happily spend a few minutes with them, and just as I say 'bye' my inner voice says, 'I told you.' I assure you this isn't multiple personality disorder, it's merely me talking to, well, me.

I think it's important we do humble ourselves on a frequent basis. People have done this all the way back to Marcus Aurelius, the stoic philosopher. Every time a citizen bowed down to greet the emperor or shouted a word of praise about his great deeds, Marcus Aurelius instructed his servant to whisper a few words in his ear. These were the words: 'You're just a man. You're just a man.' (See References, p. 263) This is of course at the opposing end of the spectrum of this book: humility can be a practice that opposes confidence, but their connection can almost be intertwined.

Naysayers and Confidence Killers

It pains me to remind you of this, but sometimes those who love you the most will try to hinder your success the most, whether they're aware of it or not. It doesn't mean their intentions are ill willed. It means they're often trying to prevent you from the pain that comes with failing. A 'naysayer' is a *person who criticises, objects to, or opposes something*. I've had best friends say to me why I shouldn't do things. I have to look at what they're saying from where they are standing – everything is relative, things are different from where you're standing compared to someone else's perspective. You don't want to see your best friends fail, that's a fact, and for a lot of your friends they're worried that what you want to do won't work out. Do not let the opinions of others hinder your attempts, you don't need their protection because you're aware how important failing is to succeed in life. Confidence isn't about being shielded from failure, quite the opposite. It's our relationship to failure. 'Confidence Killers' are what I call people who quite simply don't see the world through the same lens as some of us do. For instance, the majority of people will either have a 'scarcity' mindset or an 'abundance' mindset. This isn't fixed for everyone either. I'll add that when I began as a personal trainer I would tell myself in my head 'people can't afford to pay x'. When I look back now, I think to myself if any gym has 1,000 members, even if 1 per cent earn an amount high enough and have the desire to be fit enough, they can afford to populate your entire business: 1 per cent of 1,000 is 10, 10 people seeing you 2–3 times a week, that's a full personal training business.

The scarcity mindset sees the entire world as a cake: if someone takes a big slice of it, they just assume that means there's less for everyone else. It's why people tend to hate 'rich' people as a default. But weirdly, according to studies, people love and admire individual billionaires, but strongly dislike the class of very wealthy people, millionaires or the top 1 per cent of earners. (See References, p. 263) So, when people spot millionaires, they think they're unfairly and unjustly manipulating people for their wealth to accumulate to a certain point. They look over the fact that they could be employing dozens, hundreds or thousands of people and providing income for countless families across the world. These scarcity mindset folk will be the first to try and be a naysayer against your dreams, passions or objectives in life.

I'm not saying all wealthy people are philanthropic good people, I'm just saying there are people whose default to success is nearly hatred. I do share concerns that much of our economy does end up like a Monopoly board: players starting with the same amount of cash and opportunity (equality of opportunity) do not share the equality of outcome, so whoever gets further ahead at the outset will monopolise the economy. This again is a well-studied field, but not the purpose of this book.

Opposing the naysayer and scarcity mindset folk, you have people who share the abundance mindset and I feel it's truly imperative you surround yourself with these people the best you can.

'The quality of a person's life is most often a direct reflection of the expectations of their peer group.'

Tony Robbins, inspirational speaker

The abundance mindset is that there is enough of everything for everybody. More than enough. When I think of having the abundance mindset, I think of having limitless opportunity in absolutely anything. Whether business or life in general, you must attack opportunities with optimism. This isn't as easy as pulling yourself out of bed tomorrow proclaiming, 'Hallelujah, the glass is half full now.' It's something that needs to be trained, developed, learned and implemented. Human beings tend to lean to something known as the pessimism bias, where we do not see opportunity as 50/50 good outcome or bad outcome, we see it as more likely to be a negative outcome, unless we can train our minds to spot the pessimism bias and ignore it when it needs to be ignored. Therefore, the abundance mindset is more of a mental exercise than a default, and can become a part of your toolkit when working on building confidence.

Pessimism Bias

The pessimism bias refers to the tendency to overestimate the likelihood of negative events while underestimating the likelihood of positive events. This attitude of expecting the worst is a prominent cognitive feature of depression and can have considerable ramifications on both a personal and societal level. (See References, p. 263)

On my last book tour, I'd joke about the fact that when I get a phone call at a peculiar time, I often answer saying, 'Who died?' I think the bias is evolutionary, that's my take. I mean, if we had a pool of millions of human beings that had to survive over hundreds of thousands of years, those who were over-optimistic probably found their way out of the gene pool a lot sooner than those who saw the world slightly more pessimistically. I can only imagine a hundred thousand years ago, our early ancestors eyeballing the gap between two islands to swim across. The ones who perhaps saw the swim without any negative outcomes may not have made it to the other side, and hundreds of thousands of people would have never survived the lineage. A morbid adage, but that's my theory. A bit like the theory of why dogs are the majority of the time so loving and amazing to be around. Because over thousands of years, dogs with bad attitudes wouldn't coexist with human beings well enough to survive and thrive. Let's look at it this way, if a wild dog is an absolute arsehole to you, you're hardly going to share your leftovers with it, are you? This means that wild dogs with bad attitudes would be hugely reducing their chances of surviving. Therefore, before breeding was 'a thing', I can only imagine that it wasn't survival of the fittest for most canines, but instead survival of the best natured and best mannered dogs.

Getting to my point, I think it's ok to realise we're hardwired to see a pessimistic outcome at first, but only at first. We have the cognitive computing ability to overturn any thought that enters our mind. What if it all goes wrong? What if it all goes right? What if this is the worst decision I ever make? What if this is the best decision I ever make?

'If you look at what you have in life, you'll always have more. If you look at what you don't have in life, you'll never have enough.'

Oprah Winfrey

To conclude: in life some people see the world as a glass half empty, as a cake without enough to go around. This does not make them bad people, it just means you'll no doubt have a clash of personal values at some point. If you listen to them too much or let their stance on your dreams, goals or ambitions affect your decision-making process, you are removing yourself one step farther from where you need to be as far as the mindset for being successful goes. Confidence is predicting an outcome for success; if people dampen your belief in the outcome, they will steal and kill your confidence. Pick your passengers wisely.

We're all guilty to some respect of expecting the worst. We can all too easily hide this under the guise of anticipating and being prepared. But we should never let our mind expect the worst as a default. 'There's no point putting myself out there because she won't want to go on a date' or 'There's no point asking because I won't get a pay rise' often are just barriers we put up to avoid being uncomfortable. Surrounding yourself with the right people and keeping the right people around you plays a tremendous part in what you perceive to be possible.

Causing Offence and Criticism

When I encounter someone who I perceive to have a lack of confidence, I can always see behind it some form or element of fear, that's clear, but when really thinking about what it is that they're fearful of, for many, for so many, it's the fear of offending someone or causing offence or even worse yet, being criticised or offended themselves. Ultimately, most human beings from a psychological perspective do not want to upset other people. Because of this, there's one thing that seems to have almost evaporated from human interaction – the ability to have a difference of opinion. We do not have to have the same opinion on things, that's why we have political parties, so that people with different ideologies can oppose one another and be elected by the majority, it's the foundation of democracy. Nowadays, a differing opinion has become very polarising, in some cases people take dramatic offence to you stating your opinion. One thing I like to remind people is that you're allowed to be wrong. The world nowadays seems to think that ignorance is a sin. It's a lack of knowledge, that's quite literally the definition of 'ignorance'. We're all in some respects fearful of criticism, so how do we overcome these fears of criticism, causing offence and upsetting people while still expressing how we feel?

There is quite literally nothing you can say that won't be criticised or objected to by someone on the planet. Even saying the world is a sphere would upset some flat earthers somewhere. So this is my way of dealing with criticism and causing offence.

(Something I Want to Express or Say) x (My Personal Values) =
Saying it unapologetically

Ultimately, you need to decide what is in line with your personal values and use the equation above. If your personal values are authenticity, you will probably decide to express and say what you want. Should a bombardment of criticism come, you must use your values as a shield to protect yourself. I could get an email right now with someone upset with something I've said or expressed. I can then lean on my values and sleep at night knowing it was the right decision based on that. Of course, if your personal values are in line with not upsetting other people and maintaining a level of agreeableness, perhaps it's better you stay silent. Either way, how other people react should not be held as your problem; you must act on your own best interests and in line with your own values, without apology.

Keep in mind being wrong is ok, gaps in your knowledge are to be expected. No one is a finished product by any means. Even experts aren't always right, you just expect them to make decisions to the *best of their knowledge*, not outside of it, because of course we can't know all of what we don't know. There's something called the 'Corrective Feedback Paradigm' where failure is not seen as opposed to success but as a part of it. Failing often leads to a negative outcome, whether it's not getting your driving licence or having to re-sit an important test. But for many people failure is when they learn the most. Failure is not just a part, it's often the most impactful part of changing future behaviours and therefore outcomes. But you won't always know if you're wrong unless you say what you want to say at the time. You don't open the door to being corrected, you can't be educated by being silent. Say what you want to say. If you're right, excellent. If you're wrong, you will no doubt learn something that will benefit your position. It's not often I see a true benefit from suppressing what you want to express.

Aggression

Aggression in this context isn't wanting to fight, it's not an angry white van man shouting out the window. Aggression isn't barging shoulders with someone on purpose as you walk down the street. It's not getting wound up easily, it's not even being argumentative. Aggression is the fire that lives in the belly that is necessary to bring out every now and then. We should never live a life without aggression, we should not be brought up to be tame. We should all have fiery aggressive characters inside of us that need to be tamed every single day. We're organised apes, after all, and I think it's very important we realise this every single day we exist. When you can muster, tame and control the aggressive nature inside of you and know when to let it free and use it effectively, then you're that bit better prepared for life. I include this in this book because I think a lot of people who struggle with confidence have lost touch with their sense of aggression. Even something which could seem trivial, like someone pushing into a queue in front of you, you might say, 'Excuse me, you can go to the back of the queue like everyone else, thank you very much.' That's polite and also assertive. That aggression feels good to let out, you get a warm fuzzy feeling of adrenaline after, and you realise you're not a walkover. Let's also look into the context of our relationship with failure; this person may ignore you and remain where they are, and at this point I'd say leave it. But 99 out of 100 times that person is going to go to the back of the queue. Now this isn't a part of the book where I want confrontation, but I do want you to really develop the ability to have an uncomfortable conversation. Here's the important bit, whether they go to the back of the queue or they don't. You. Have. Still. Won. You took control of the fire in the belly and used it for what was the right thing to do. I'll be honest and admit to something, sometimes when I witness someone pushing in or being rude in public, I imagine there are hidden cameras, you know, like sometimes people set up situations to see how other people react and put it on TV. There's a famous one of two girls (who are actresses) being rude to a third girl (another actress) in a gym. A man overhears what's being said and steps in and defends the girl. He in my eyes was a hero. No one was watching and he stepped in and stood up for the stranger. I sometimes like to think there are always cameras and you always have the opportunity to be the hero. Again, I'll reiterate, the outcome is out of your control. But the ability to muster the aggression inside to do the right thing is of utmost importance. Not violence, not being impolite, but standing up for the right thing. Please never underestimate the impact this has on other areas of your life. If you think doing your first chin-up was good for your confidence, imagine what sending a rude person to the back of the supermarket queue can do for you.

Aggression is what you muster at the gym. You're tired, the sets of weights are really fatiguing you and bringing your energy levels down, so you look in the mirror, you lock eyes on yourself and pull yourself together. For anyone wondering why there are so many mirrors in the gym, I can only imagine it's for a few reasons. One is to make the room look bigger, this is utilised in almost all modern fit-outs. There is the functional aspect for bodybuilders too, to ensure they're moving right, to get visual feedback on the movement, to critique their movement in real time and to remain focused on the contraction essential to the lift. However, one purpose that I think is overlooked is to give yourself the introspective talking to that you need. There's telling someone something, then there's locking eyes with them and telling them. Mirrors give us the ability to look into our own soul before going to war with a working set. Don't be disillusioned, if you want muscle to grow, you need to go to war with it. Once you've said to yourself what you need to do, you pick up your weights and you get the last remaining set fucking done. Aggression is the voice in your head that says, 'Let's go!', it's the voice that says get the fuck up the second your alarm goes off. Aggression is the part of your mind that's ready for whatever the repercussions are of the email you just sent to your boss, or the message you sent to your partner, saying 'we need to talk' about the fact they are being an arsehole in the relationship. Aggression can welcome uncertain situations and it can give you the confidence to get yourself out of tricky situations, because aggression is the fight you have inside of you. We all have it, some of us have just been deconditioned to think it's not there anymore. Channelling aggression is a big part in remaining calm, channelling aggression is an energy system sports scientists don't study deeply enough.

This is another reason why I love martial arts. So many people live their day-to-day life suppressing their inner aggressive chimp. Martial artists give this aggression a ruleset, sprinkle it with respect and make it an artform you can express. I love the idea of weaponising my abilities through martial arts with the deep-down desire to never use it. I get asked about jiu-jitsu for self-defence and to be honest I hate the idea of self-defence. Every person reading this has a certain competence to be combative with another human, whether striking, wrestling or even the ability to run away. You either develop those skills or you don't. To practise something to avoid bad things happening defines extrinsic motivation and I don't think that's a good reason to train at all. You don't inspire someone obese to lose weight by saying, 'Do this or you'll die of a heart attack.' To ignite passion you open a world to them where they find something personally rewarding; intrinsic motivation gets people out of bed in the morning, not the idea of bad things not happening.

'It is better to be a warrior in a garden than a gardener in a war.'

Chinese Proverb

There is a voice in your head that wants you to stop running when it gets tough, to sleep in, to not ask for a pay rise and to tolerate average working conditions. There's a voice in your head that says, 'Next Monday I'll start' and that 'I can't' this and 'I can't' that. You'll need to find your inner aggression to ignore these voices so you can finally get all the shit done that you need to. This isn't going to be easy for a lot of you and there is often work to be done to really up your levels of aggression. Testosterone is a key player in this feeling, so ensure you're fit, active, sleeping well and getting enough Vitamin D through sunlight or supplementation. Don't forget your best supplementation is to implement more health seeking behaviours in your life, don't believe for a second that positive changes to your body won't lead to positive changes in your life.

Imagine an internal combustion engine: the methods and principles I talk about in this book is the aspirated fuel going into the cylinder ready to be ignited. The aggression you muster inside of you is the spark that causes the engine to fire, creating movement and progression. You need an optimal amount of both, in order to move forward. No good having adequate fuel without a spark or having the spark but no fuel to ignite it.

Travelling Confidence

Right at the beginning of my career I used to completely make up things I was being asked in order to create some reason to post on certain topics. When it came to being confident at the beginning of a LIVE Q&A, what better way than to pretend I'd been asked something: 'You guys keep asking me about intermittent fasting, so …' I'd quite literally get my tripod out, set it all up, press 'go live' then reel off the answers to about five topics I'd pre-rehearsed and make it seem like I was being asked. This did two things, it allowed me to populate the video before genuine questions were asked. On top of that, it then gave people a reason to actually ask them. About three months into making up questions, I genuinely received enough to actually answer at the outset. So, a quick footnote for public speaking: If you need a good way to begin, invent a kind of dialogue with the audience that you've essentially made up. Make sure you're speaking on topics you're well versed on and it will not only make you look like a natural, but you'll feel more like one too.

But I'll be honest with you now, one question I get asked a hell of a lot is about 'finding the confidence' to travel, especially to travel solo. I suppose the norm is set that you travel with people, the status quo is to travel in a group or a partnership and/or relationship. To travel solo is almost frowned upon.

I know there are safety concerns for solo travel, especially with women, and I suppose the context of where you're travelling to is going to impact that. But many people want to travel but they are not confident enough to do it alone, held back by a fear that they can't do it, or it won't work out or even worse yet, they won't enjoy it. I am experienced in travelling and going solo is by far my favourite method, you are almost pressurised to speak to people, to make friends and to go up to a group of people and ask, 'Hey, can I join you guys? I'm travelling here on my own.' Every time people smiled and said yes; of course in my head I thought every time they would be hostile and unwilling of my company but when you travel solo, like I think a lot of people do, you share this sense of joined vulnerability that makes the bonding between travellers even tighter. Like the wolves, the numbers are always greater until they are counted. You can bet that the majority of your fears of travelling solo are much bigger and greater in your mind than they ever are in reality.

I've travelled all of South-East Asia with a partner before; in hindsight it was great for many things, but terrible for others. When travelling solo, you can sometimes quite simply have enough of some people and you want to move on; when you've had enough of your girlfriend, that becomes a lot tougher, I can tell you that first-hand. When you travel in a partnership, you set sail with a lot less fear and you're going to feel more confident for sure as you're with someone you know and trust. The only downside to this is you often become a bit siloed off from the groups, as it's a lot easier to go do your own thing than immerse yourself in the crowds. Young readers of this book, think carefully if you're going to travel with a partner. If you're doing it just to avoid awkward conversations with strangers, you're missing the opportunity to not only develop your travel skills, but you'll miss out on enjoying the best part of meeting and socialising with new people. If you're an older reader, make sure your kids don't make the same mistake I did. My mum told me before I left, 'James, you're making a bad decision travelling with your girlfriend.' She was, as always, bloody right.

I think the best way to frame the argument to anyone thinking about it, is to do this. Think to yourself, 'If I had all the confidence in the world, would I travel solo or with my partner?' If you still think you would, by all means do it, but if you think you're doing it just to play the game safely, you're going to miss the best parts of it. Stretching comfort zones while travelling are going to be some of the best experiences of your life, I went to Coachella in 2019 with three girls I'd never met before, I've travelled to America on my own, Fiji, Bali, around Europe and I even went to Australia completely on my own … and it was fantastic. It's worth noting that you do need to train yourself at travelling on your own, see it like a new workout you haven't done before, the first day, the day after and so forth; as the stimulus is completely new, it will feel pretty intense and even slightly uncomfortable. Solo travelling has been incredible for my own mental growth. I am forced into uncomfortable situations, meeting new people and no one will tell you how much more you can read, think, ponder and even listen to audiobooks and podcasts on drives in a shitty, cheap rental car. I know what you're thinking, you're thinking, 'But James, you've taught us about the survivorship bias, we can see it clearly. You're just expressing your emotions because you went travelling solo and you survived all those trips to come out saying it was great solo.' I concede, partially true. But drawing on experiences of other travellers I know, I think solo is where the magic happens; it's in my eyes the pinnacle of self-development. There is no other word to describe some experiences than beautiful. You walk the streets of somewhere you never expected to end up in your life. Sunglasses on, headphones in, random playlist. You wander around with no expectations and you stumble across a little place to eat, you sit, have a coffee and open your book. Any human being within 50 feet could end up being the best man at your wedding, your future wife or just a lover for the evening, perhaps a future business partner or just another human being you lock eyes with and never ever see again.

Another reason people lack confidence with travelling and the fear surrounding it can be the cost. Now loss aversion will try and kick your butt at every opportunity, but I think you need to consider the cost of not travelling, of not seeking adventures in your life. Or like I said for the older readers, what is the cost of your children not travelling? Whether in a hostel in Cairns, a hire car on Route 66 or a train journey across Europe in a TGV train, there is something incredible about taking the risks of travelling and the growth that comes as a part of it. Solo travel also brings about a lot more of what would have been known as 'dead time' before the internet. But audiobooks, self-help books, podcasts and general media on the internet can now fill that space; days where you have no plans you can sit, be still and absorb from these sources. I know that having the confidence to up and leave everything I had with very limited savings was one of the best decisions I've ever made. I acquired time to learn, read and build a business because of it. The time advantage you have travelling solo is something that cannot be really fathomed until you have experienced it.

A young lad asked me at one of my events what he should do with £10,000 he inherited. I said, 'Go travelling for a few months, read some books, stay in hostels, meet new people and try to decide what you want to do with your life.' The ability to take a break from life to think about these things would be worth a hell of a lot more than the money itself. Loss aversion would hinder most people's ability to spend inheritance money, it's hard to let go of, a bit like the mug and the chocolate bar. Even though not long ago you had nothing, the idea of giving up something feels a lot more psychologically painful than the idea of what you could gain, that gain being some perspective on your life, values and future. Isn't it crazy that you'd feel the pain of spending the £10,000 having the best time of your life, even though you got it completely free?

> *'And then there is the most dangerous risk of all – the risk of spending your life not doing what you want on the bet you can buy yourself the freedom to do it later.'*
>
> Randy Komisar, *The Monk and the Riddle: The Education of a Silicon Valley Entrepreneur*

If you're someone who's considering sacking it all off and travelling the world a bit, it's not a decision really, is it? Because your mind is already made up, let's not beat around the bush here. If you're thinking about it most days, the reality is you're fully decided, you're just behind a firewall of fear. You're waiting for someone, for me perhaps, to make it less scary for you. You're wanting it to be less scary instead of finding the courage you should be seeking to just do it, just go. For so many of the scariest decisions in life, it's about jumping in and correcting the course along the route.

What if it all goes wrong? What if it all goes right? What if it's the worst decision you'll ever make?

What if … it's the best decision you'll ever make?

What if … it's the best decision you'll **ever** make?

Dating, Alcohol and Confidence

Remember in the first part of the book I said, 'If we could bottle up confidence.' Well, we're not far away from it when it comes to alcohol. Alcohol has a big part to play in many cultures, not all of them, but many of them. It has a reputation for helping people with courage or confidence, known as 'Dutch courage' in some regards. In the Cambridge dictionary, Dutch courage is defined as 'the confidence that some people get from drinking alcohol before they do something that needs courage'. If you look at alcohol's biggest roles in modern-day lives it's used as a social lubricant, something to bring people together and reduce inhibitions between them.

Inhibitions may be things from social anxiety in big groups, nerves on a first date, stuttering in an interview or generally any situation of unease. When we look at dating, for instance, there's going to be nerves and anxiety from both sides, this is completely normal when strangers are meeting for the first time. In modern times dating apps are a common place for people to 'meet', this means their first interaction is not the most natural means, so I think there's going to be more, not less, chances of heightened inhibitions as time progresses.

- ► 18 per cent of couples met their present or most recent partner through work.
- ► 50 per cent of single Britons have never asked anyone on a date in person.
- ► 25 to 29-year-olds are most likely to meet a partner on a dating app.

- ► The UK dating app market contributes around £11.7 billion to the UK economy.
- ► Almost 70 per cent of British adults think a pub or bar is the best place for a first date. (See References, p. 263)

When you look at these statistics, it's understandable why so many people would want to lean on alcohol to reduce inhibitions in a dating scene. People would rather buy a bit of confidence in a glass or a bottle, albeit only lasting a few hours, than they would want to work on their own self-esteem, their own perception of themselves or accept the fact there could be work that needs to be done on themselves. Go to your nearest shop, your nearest high street, how far do you need to walk to grab a glass or a bottle of confidence? Not far, is it any wonder true confidence is at such an all-time low when bottled confidence is everywhere, even on trains, planes and almost every restaurant in the country you live in?

To kickstart 2021, I didn't drink for six months. This was huge for me, because alcohol has been a major part of my life since I was young. I played rugby for 15 years and if you'd asked me in my mid-twenties, I'd have said my drinking team had a rugby problem. I sat back and said to my close friends and business partners that I wanted a well-needed break from alcohol. Why? Well, I wanted a better insight into why I was drinking so frequently and what I was gaining from it. Had alcohol become a proxy for me not wanting to put myself in awkward situations? Why had social drinking become such a big part of the norm? Was it my way of bottling a confidence issue? (pardon the pun).

The first thing that straightaway became more difficult was dating. I was 32, single and I needed to be dating, I needed to be putting myself out there. I've been guilty of using apps and then again been very successful at times without dating apps. I went through periods of heavy reliance and then deleting them as I thought deep down the right person for me probably wasn't swiping on an app, they'd rather a more organic means of meeting. Again this was completely fabricated in my mind; in hindsight, surely success metrics need to be set upon compatibility, not what means you used to end up meeting.

If we break down the real reasons as to why people use apps, it's 100 per cent 'fear of rejection'. It's easy to hide this fear under the guise of convenience, or to say you're too busy. But, essentially it's a means of connecting with only people who are already interested in you on a physical and I suppose superficial level. It's almost like working in sales with leads that are already considered warm, it's a much more enjoyable environment but you very soon become conditioned to the warm leads and unconditioned to the cold ones. This I think can be detrimental to the skills required to talk to someone. If we are to see confidence as a skill, it diminishes when using dating apps as there's no need for us to be conditioned to the stimuli of awkward conversations, similar to the atrophy that occurs when a muscle is not used.

Embarrassment 101: defined as 'a feeling of self-consciousness, shame, or awkwardness'. Now I don't have a magical solution to make this go away, but what I want you to think about is this. Could a change in success metrics help you deal with embarrassment? People are embarrassed of rejection, but if you set your sights of success as just doing what you're thinking about doing, you may get rejected, you may not, but you can succeed with your own metrics. When knocking on doors for a living, I didn't make it all about successful encounters, I made it about knocking on doors. I promised myself I'd knock on at least 200 doors each day, come rain or shine, sales or being shunned. Without knowing the outcome of what was to come, I knew I was capable of my success metrics. This helped me back then and even now helps me manage the feelings and emotions that come with embarrassment.

I know during this chapter you might be thinking, 'Bloody hell, James, this isn't a book for single people.' I get that, but I think that when you're partnered with someone, especially a life partner, that you'd be certainly more confident through life as a duo. I can't write chapters that suit every person like a bespoke suit. There are so many parallels to be drawn from dating and the barriers and hurdles that single people encounter. It's crazy how connected dating and marketing are in my mind. Much of the confidence people feel they lack genuinely comes from an inability to market themselves in dating, professional life and all places in between. I can't help but think that confidence is a bigger issue for people who are yet to meet a compatible partner. As much as we'd like to ignore the fact for much of our lives, we're very sociable beings and we have needs, one of which is to be in serving relationships with other people. When I say 'serving', I mean that you have support, someone to share your life with, the ups and the downs, the good and the bad. You can have all the money in the world, but if you have no one to share it with you're not going to be truly content with your time on this spinning rock moving through the Milky Way. That's my belief anyway.

Again, if some of my ideas in this book don't fully resonate with you, don't skim past them too fast, they could help someone close to you in life in the near future. Carry some of the knowledge not for your own sake, but to help those around you. I really enjoy reading parts of books

I know won't serve me, but they'll serve others. I've read books on menopause, not because it's something I'll personally deal with, but women around me will and that's what makes the chapters so important, to pass on the information to people around me.

The Utility of Deprivation

I'll never forget listening to Jordan B Peterson talk about the 'utility of deprivation', something that I'd never heard of before. Jordan spoke about how nowadays any man can expose himself to more nude women in a day than a man could previously ever do in a lifetime. I have often reflected on how this availability to information and media has so many upsides to our society and development, I then think about Newton's law about every action having an opposite reaction. Surely with all the benefits to society there must be a downside to finding all this availability of information, media, etc.? I am forever grateful that whenever I have a random thought, I can just ask Siri on my phone and have an answer within seconds. But then what are the true implications to having things satisfy our deeper urges within minutes? To quote Peterson, he said, 'Don't substitute the false for the real, don't underestimate the utility of deprivation.'

When we are deprived of something, I like to imagine a building of pressure inside the mind that causes some form of action. When the pressure builds to a certain point, the desire to take action will get to the point where the anxiety behind not doing it loses momentum to the pressure to do it. In some areas of our life, we could seek deprivation to build hunger towards it. This doesn't have to be permanent either, but if you're relying on dating apps or pornography it could be worth depriving yourself of them to see if it positively impacts your actions. When I first arrived in Sydney in 2016, a good friend of mine made me delete my dating apps. I was reluctant at first, as I'd relied heavily on Tinder to keep some 'companionship', let's say, while travelling down the east coast of Australia.

I still remember clearly the girl I met at the rooftop party, the date I organised on the bus home one day and the times I left my number on a napkin in a café. There was no greater feeling knowing I'd done something that I was, up until recently, quite terrified of. The dates felt better to be on, almost more organic if that even makes sense. I also had a nice thought in my mind that if it did work out and she was 'the one' that it would make a good story for my kids saying I met their mother on a bus one day and I was brave enough to ask for her number. However, thinking back to these times, I must have written my number down wrong in several situations, because I never heard back from some. I'm only joking, in a way I'd already won the moment by asking, and that's the point I really want people to take from this book. I'd already taken the victory from putting myself out there; if I got a message or not was almost irrelevant. I had substituted the false for the real and I won't lie, it felt much better every time.

I'm not saying that everyone should join the NoFap movement (of abstaining from masturbation and pornography). But I am asking you to consider the implications of these things on your behaviour. Every action has a reaction, every inaction and action has consequences further down the line. So, as I close out this chapter, I ask you to think about this: is there anything in your life that you're bypassing the deprivation of? Could your reliance on technology, whether dating apps, emailing instead of calling, whatever it is, could this be keeping you from the very point you need in life to overcome the anxiety of it going wrong, and actually doing it? If you deleted the apps, what actions would have to happen? Would that benefit your situation? Having your back against the wall in these situations is more of a superpower than a hindrance, I promise you that.

Chapter 7

Visualisation → Actualisation

It's important that we consider visualisation in connection with what I discussed about manifestation in Part One; to put it simply, the reason we need to envisage things going well is so that they actually can go well. Visualisation is essentially a hidden weapon that allows you to practise situations internally – it's a learning opportunity that many don't make full use of, and people don't reap the advantages that can come from it.

When I played rugby, my position in the forwards meant I was very likely to catch the ball from the kick-off. Catching a ball is not the hardest skill, but doing this with 15 opposition players running at you as fast as they can, that's a lot more difficult. The kicker will hoof the ball up to a tremendous height, so as I stand there to catch the opposing team's kick I am staring into the sun while simultaneously trying to gauge the ball's direction, trajectory, hang time and wind direction. Anyone who has been on a volleyball court will know Newton's Fifth Law of Height = Time. Ok, I'm joking, Newton never said that, but he should have. So the higher the ball, the more time the opposition has to close the gap on me catching it. Now mix this in with the pressure of the game, the score, my family watching from the sidelines, there is a certain amount of anxiety you'd feel. This isn't a rule across every player either when it comes to performance. So let's quickly discuss why differing levels of anxiety can hinder or help your performance.

Introducing the Inverted U Hypothesis

'A little excitement and stress associated with a competition can have a positive effect, but a situation that is too stressful is detrimental. However, the optimal levels of arousal vary between people doing the same task.'

Yerkes, R.M. & Dodson, J. D.' (See References, p. 263)

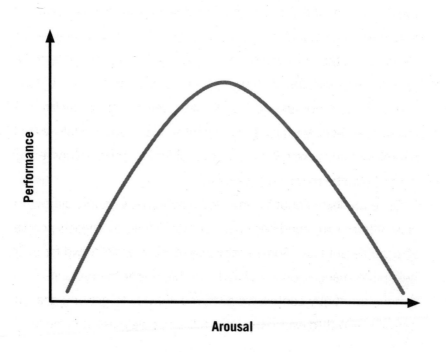

Imagine yourself doing a complex task. Then imagine how you'd perform with no one watching; how you may perform with a small group watching; then with a stadium watching. The onlookers would create different amounts of 'arousal' anxiety. The reason I include this in the book is because I'm sure the amount of people looking at your act, habit, sport or social situation that requires a certain level of confidence will have an influential impact. Should the bar be busy, or there are more interviewers listening than you expected, you will soon have a hypothesis to lean back on to understand why not all of your performances are the same. A weird fact for you is that I find small crowds make me very nervous and larger crowds put me at ease. My inverted U would look significantly different to anyone else's, I am sure. When I talk to a bigger crowd, say 500 to 1,000 people, it's impossible to truly appreciate how many individuals are in the room. I can't really lock eyes with someone like I would in a crowd of 50. I also take personal pleasure in the amount of people there. A bit like John Travolta saying, 'You've done the work.' Knowing I'm speaking in front of 1,000 people is a real-time indication that my efforts have paid off, the work is done and it's time to go out and yes, perform well, but to appreciate the moment and enjoy it. I have every right to worry about a talk when I haven't sold any tickets. But when the room is full, it's time to just enjoy it. The crowd helps me do that, weirdly.

Once you learn about the inverted U hypothesis it's very difficult to erase it from your mind because of how it differently impacts people across different tasks. Some rugby players need a big crowd for their best performances, others would crumble under the pressure. Let's remove the rugby context for a second. If I was to go for a deadlift personal record, I'd want a big room full of people pressuring me to lift it, screaming 'let's go!' and slapping me on the back. However, for a more complex task like writing this book, I may prefer there to be less arousal, none in fact. Usually, it's a café where I can sit in the corner, left completely alone. I tend not to even write in the house because my housemates are much more likely to unapologetically interrupt me than someone would in a café when I have my headphones on and I'm in the zone. Something to think about when you think of your own levels of arousal: there is an optimal amount for different tasks within your life, some high, some low, and the better you understand that the better you will perform.

Back to the moments after the rugby ball has been drop-kicked high in the air. My frame of mind is very important here, the game could quite literally rely on it. So I did on that last kick-off what I had done since being a young whippersnapper on the field in my early teens, I played out the scenario in my head over and over. I think of all scenarios in my head. I catch it, I catch it well. I think about which side it's kicked, if I have to move forward, back, left, right, and I catch it in my head over and over. I would listen to music on the bus to away games and just drift my mind to many scenarios, getting in the extra reps of catching with my mind. I'd then think about lineouts, I'd think about scrums, I'd like to imagine every scenario. To me, I used each imaginative experience as a way to build up my confidence. The catches may not have been real, but to me they were. The bus was a good place to think about it, but the best time was out on the pitch where I could build it up in the exact place it would take place. I could look at the surroundings, feel the breeze, the temperature, the wind, everything. Personally, I think it's best if you recreate as much as possible for the ideal situation of visualisation. If you're going to prepare for an interview in the mirror at home, no harm in having the suit on so you can get a feel for the exact moments about to play out. I'll do the same on the stage. As I'm standing in front of hundreds of empty seats, I fill the seats with my imagination and play out the different parts of the talk dozens of times before the doors even open.

I do the same with jiu-jitsu, I imagine myself getting the takedown or the move which I desire, I play it out in my mind and visualise it. You'd be amazed how much your mental reps benefit your ability to do something. Don't get me wrong, it didn't save me from every kick on the rugby field, especially not on rainy days, but I am positive it benefited me in some capacity for future situations. I have spoken in front of crowds bigger than a thousand people dozens of times and if you were to ask me if I am nervous before I go on stage, the answer is not really, not half as much as you'd expect. One of the reasons is that although the amount of times I've been on stage is in the dozens, the amount of accrued mental reps of the situation is in the hundreds, maybe even the thousands. For many, meditation is about clearing the mind, for me it's sometimes about filling the mind with many repetitions of whatever I need to develop or become more experienced at. I use these practices to control my levels of arousal. Should I not practise the scenarios, I will no doubt be over-aroused and emotions will get the better of me. Thinking about the situation and all of its outcomes not only readies me on a psychological basis, but in a genuine physiological readiness too. There are plenty of times to get your reps in speaking publicly, talking to a stranger, asking for a pay rise or whatever it may be, but the ability to do the reps in your imagination is one of the most important tools you can use.

'Imagery (Visualisation) has become one of the most popular psychological techniques to improve performance in athletic, academic, and work contexts. Imagery is especially well studied in sports, and research in that area supports the claim that imagery improves a wide range of relevant, beneficial outcomes such as objective performance, exercise frequency, attentional focus, game-related tension, and confidence, but also a quicker recovery from injury – outcomes that have been examined across a range of sports contexts.'

Tim Blankert and Melvyn R. W. Hamstra (See References, p. 263)

There is a specific imagery technique called PETTLEP that is considered most effective and is currently most prominent. The acronym indicates that physical, environment, task, timing, learning, emotional, and perspective relevant aspects of the imagery all need to be aligned with the aspects of the actual activity. This means the physical state (e.g. the clothes and attributes), the environment (e.g. the playing field), the specific movements involved in the actual activity, and the speed of the actual activity all need to be the same as in the actual movement. Further, the athlete should adapt the imagery to his or her current skill level, to experience the emotions he or she would experience in a game situation, and finally to view the situation from his or her own perspective, as it would be seen if he or she was to carry out the activity him- or herself.

You can understand now why racing drivers walk the track, why performers do their own sound checks, etc. Because visualising what's to come will genuinely benefit the outcome.

Let's imagine you've got a job interview coming up. You'll want to do your research on the business and also the role, you may even script how you would answer certain questions. One of the hardest questions I've ever had to face was, 'So why should we hire you over anyone else applying for this job?' The first time I was asked, I did what anyone would do, I froze, my eyes became wide open and for one of only a handful of occasions in my life I became speechless. Knowing what you're going to say in my opinion isn't enough; merely the words or the structure of the sentence isn't enough to really convince someone. When I utilise visualisation I must also dial-in how I say it, how I present it, what gestures I use, where I look, how I am sitting or even how I am standing. There are many more variables than just the words that are said. Whenever I go on TV, I always have a rough idea of 4–5 topics I'll get asked, so as I drive in my car I answer them over and over again. I say them how I'd like to say them and with every repetition of me saying it, I hone-in the tone, the pitch and the speed of how I say certain points, how I emphasise certain areas and perfect it over time. You can YouTube something incredibly rare that happened on Live TV: I got Piers Morgan to say, 'I completely agree with you James.' There's probably only two or three people in the world who have heard that from Piers himself. If you watch the interview on *Good Morning Britain* you'd easily think I was born good at speaking or answering questions. You didn't see my flight I took home from Ireland the night before, I left all my best friends in Dublin on a whim that I might be on TV the next day. They didn't even speculate that I'd have a 50 per cent chance of being on TV, but I left anyway. I spent the hour on the flight scribbling responses to questions I might be asked. You didn't see the 35 minutes I spent at 6 a.m. in front of a mirror in some dodgy hotel in

Shepherd's Bush reciting 'Well, Piers, the thing is this …' Those reps didn't just prepare me, they readied me for the biggest interview of my life and I sold enough hardbacks off the interview alone to obtain one of the highest accolades possible for an author that should be on the front of this very book you're reading.

I hope by briefly checking the cover of the book just then, you'll appreciate the potential of visualisation. I'm not saying that mental reps is enough to get Piers Morgan to agree with you, but I am making a strong point that visualisation (to me) is an incredibly powerful tool. It's powerful because I can build up in my mind the room, the interviewer, the tricky questions, the handshake, the small talk. Every single component of what is a pretty intimidating feat can be practised before it even happens. I conducted an epilogue on my last book tour which is probably the most powerful three minutes of speaking I've ever done in my life so far. During the epilogue, I had the sound technicians play 'Time' by Hans Zimmer, to me this song brings an immense intensity to whatever vocals are presented to it, hence its popularity in online motivation videos over the years. The epilogue was about something that's very personal to me, it's a fallacy known as the 'end of history illusion'. So whenever footage circulates of me backstage before a big speaking event, you'll see me with my headphones in and I bet you can guess what exactly I'm listening to. As I play the background song to myself, I think about what to say, how I'm going to say it, I visualise where I walk, how I stand and how I present what is potentially life-changing information to those who have attended to hear it. I close my eyes, I put myself standing where I am and I recite what to say, how to say it, when to pause, when not to. Like the thousands of reps it takes to be competent doing an Olympic lift, I'm doing my warm-up sets in my mind, to ready myself, breaking down nerves and fears with repetitions and positive outcomes, creating an optimal amount of arousal to allow a peak performance on not only the inverted U hypothesis, but the stage or talk I'm about to perform.

Let's imagine any scenario, first date, getting someone's number, presenting a pitch, recording a bit of video content for social media, whatever it is. The actual event doesn't need to be the first attempt. You can use your mind to visualise so many variations of the scenario before you put yourself into it. I know a few of you reading this may be feeling sceptical about this, but in researching its efficacy it proves to be a method that actually works. Basketball players have been tested on their free throw performances in training and in games and found a heightened performance in successful throws from visualising the scenarios beforehand. (See References, p. 263)

Now this isn't to say that all you need to do is think your way through any scenario, but it's a means of completing mental reps before execution. It may not bring you a 100 per cent success rate, I don't think anything does, but wherever you stand I'm confident that seeing the scenario through a few times in your mind will bring you closer to succeeding. I've divulged a lot of secrets in this book, so here's another. If you go back to a lot of my videos on social media, I get a lot of questions as to why my hair can look wet a lot of the time. I shower before most important videos I film to give myself 5–10 minutes to do the mental reps and visualisation practice necessary to get my point across in the best manner possible. Next time you need to create something important or present yourself, I'd recommend a distraction-free shower. (I would say a 5 to10-minute lie down but I'm prone to naps, so I'm better off in the shower.)

Public Speaking: My Hacks Exposed

I'll be honest with you. I've been what feels like completely winging most of my career and somehow I went from an ambitious personal trainer, who was quite happy on the gym floor doing 5–7 hours of personal training a day, to a TED speaker, director of a seven-figure business and bestselling author in quite literally a handful of years. I sit in fancy meeting rooms with expensive accountants and lawyers, I nod away, and the majority of the time things go right over my head. But I think it's a good idea to explain how I got started in the public speaking space. So rewind back to 2017. I'm in what can only be described as my 'peak winging' period. I'm sitting in my apartment on Bondi beach in Sydney, it's April which means the weather is beginning to cool down. I haven't seen my parents in a few months, so I think to myself what a bloody good idea it would be to create a work event out of thin air, I'd host it in the UK, then fly back to it and expense the flights. In this peak winging period, I'm not even sure I fully grasped what would be acceptable as a business cost, nor did I fully realise that 'business expenses' doesn't mean it's free. I wish my friends knew that to this day, they seem to think if it's on the business, it's free.

I enquire about a hotel near where I used to personal train in a physical gym, I book out a meeting room for the day and bosh, I put the event on Facebook and send a few marketing emails. Forty-eight hours pass and … shit the bed … I've sold 180 tickets to my first ever solo speaking gig. What was I speaking about? I had no idea at this point. But surely you're better to sell the tickets then prepare the talk than vice versa, in fact, that's your first lesson in public speaking already: sell

190

the event first then worry about what you're going to do after. Fun fact for you while we're here. Did you know they pick the smell last when creating perfume and aftershave? They create the brand, the bottle, the colours used and then they need to find a smell that matches the brand. I suggest you do the same when you're considering what to speak about. By all means, do your market research, ensure people want to come to the talk. I named my UK talk the 'fundamentals of fat loss' or something similar; the majority of my clients came to me for fat loss so it made sense. Come to think of it, 180 people, that's a lot.

Any idea as to what the largest group of people I'd spoken in front of before this was? Five. So a 36-fold increase in attendees, I best prepare my talk to mitigate any chances of a refund, which brings me on to public speaking lesson number two: If you're truly terrified about speaking publicly, a massive part of that will be worrying about letting down the attendees, right? If you're that worried, offer every attendee a money-back guarantee from your speaking event, if you're hosting it, that is. From a business perspective, the money-back guarantee will get you more extra sales than refunds. This gives you an almost bullet-proof perspective on your talk: if you don't like it, you don't pay. Not many things in life give you that, the next film you go to see at the cinema won't even offer that.

Even the most elite of speakers you'll tend to see will use a presenta-tion. Now let me let you in on probably the biggest secret of public speaking: the presentation is 80 per cent there for you, 20 per cent for them. That will take some getting used to, but appreciate that the presentation allows you to do your thing more than anything. If I was to ask you to talk about something for 20 minutes, it's terrifying right? How about for 1 minute? Not so scary, ok, what if I asked you to speak about something you're well versed on for 1 minute? That's not hard. How about 2 things, for 1 minute each separately? See where I am going? With a presentation you could have 20 topics which you explain for 1 minute each. The thing about memory is we have a finite capacity to remember things. The average person can hold a set of about 7 digits in his/her working memory at any given time. (See References, p. 263) That is a lot but also not even enough for a phone number; our mind is very complex and it's mind boggling that you can remember the entire map on *Grand Theft Auto* or the lyrics to your favourite song that is 3 minutes long, but a phone number gives you the same memory as a goldfish. That's not fair on goldfish to be fair, because apparently they actually can remember things up to 5 months later. (See References, p. 263)

When it comes to presenting, it's about breaking down your talk into categories, then spreading those out on slides and then working through each one. The slide just needs to jog your memory to remember, that's it. Have you ever seen a comedian on stage do a 1-hour comedy special without checking their notes? Well, in many cases there is a monitor just in front of their feet, sometimes this will display as little as one word to nudge the memory of the comedian to which joke they're going to from the previous. Many times, the sip of water they take is to gather their thoughts and look at the monitor before moving on, even the break to grab a sip lets their mind recoup and gather information for the next part, something you can do when public speaking too. So all a comedian needs to know is the next joke; all you need to know is the next subject, you don't even have to remember it until you press the clicker to the next slide. Some things like statistics can be difficult to remember, so the beauty of presenting those is that the audience needs them too. Remember 80 per cent for you, 20 per cent for them. The last final golden rule I'll remind you of in this chapter is: when presenting, selling, pitching whatever it is, *you're always better off leaving them wanting more, than giving them too much.* Feel free to read that again before moving to the next section.

Communication

Communication isn't just with other people, it's really important that people understand we communicate on an ongoing basis with ourselves. I believe that aspirations are born from conversations we have with ourselves. The Oxford dictionary defines aspiration as 'a hope or ambition of achieving something'. It's time for you to use your imagination; we're going to use a bit of self-talk to enable you to understand what is beyond your limitations. So let's imagine for a second that tonight before you go to bed I give you a pill, or a potion or whatever you think is appropriate. Tomorrow, you wake up with the perfect amount of confidence, nothing will faze you, nothing will get in your way. How would you feel? How would you act? What would you wear? How would things be different to how they are now?

What is interesting here is that these questions pose you with answers that aren't limited to how you see your limitations now. The narrative which we hold and communicate internally is very much a story we tell ourselves on a daily basis. Human beings have been fantastic storytellers for years; without good stories I'm sure civilisation would be very different to how it is today. Think about it, to get 10,000 men to go to war, what you really need is a good story to make them want to go. It's important that the story we hold about ourselves doesn't become a fairytale which they all too often can be. When we connect our own dots and miss out the tough times, it's all too easy to believe our own stories. This is when our ego holds the conversation in our mind and hijacks the route of confident thinking.

'If ego is the voice that tells us we're better than we really are, we can say ego inhibits true success by preventing a direct and honest connection to the world around us.'

Ryan Holiday, *Ego Is the Enemy*

Keeping our ego in check is going to be a big part in ensuring confidence doesn't become arrogance. The Merriam-Webster dictionary defines arrogance as 'an attitude of superiority manifested in an overbearing manner or in presumptuous claims or assumptions'. We don't want that. We want to remove limitations to our mind when imagining a utopian world where we have unlimited confidence, but we don't want to manifest arrogance in the process. When I think about my own story, it could be all so easy to get caught up in the successes with books, events and other things, but I always ensure I connect the dots with the not so sexy things that can get forgotten when storytelling to ourselves. The 4:45 a.m. alarm, the years of starting work at 6 a.m., the years of doing 10 hours of PT a day, the countless times eating with my parents utterly exhausted and not wanting to engage in conversation because I'd been doing it all day with clients. It's very easy for people to let their imagination conjure their brilliance or their abilities, but it's essential we remember the stress, the sacrifice and the work that went into our successes. This is how you remain humble when setting your aspirations as high as they possibly could ever be.

Our aspirations must align with our values. It's important that we recognise that our inspirations and aspirations are not unique or original, we have inherited them from other people's actions that we've been exposed to. We need to ensure that our aspirations align with our personal values too. You can't take on someone else's aspirations and make them your own all the time. For instance, in my generation I see a lot of young people setting their benchmark of success on owning a home. There's absolutely nothing wrong with that. But I can sense that a lot of the time they're trying to fulfill someone else's aspirations, often the parents and not their own, and can feel rather empty after accomplishing the aspiration of purchasing a home. So when communicating with yourself about your true aspirations and making the sky the limit, you must ensure they're your aspirations and not ones passed down to you. Following someone else's dream that you don't believe in will make everything seem like an uphill battle. I've encountered this hundreds if not thousands of times with fitness and personal training; most people who want a six-pack are living life holding someone else's aspirations at the front of their mind. If they hadn't been exposed to so much media of people in the top 0.1 per cent of physical condition, they wouldn't want a six-pack. They'd want to feel good, perform well and get stronger. It's very hard and very restrictive to get someone so lean that their six-pack is on show. So it doesn't take long for that person to become disheartened on the journey there. Then people label them as failures and that they do not want it enough. The reality is more in line with the fact that people often without knowing it are aspiring to have someone else's end goal that doesn't align with their values. I believe this vast exposure to other people's aspirations, whether physical, financial or any other, is hindering the levels of confidence among millions of people on a daily basis. They see the end point as a six-pack or to be a millionaire; to not be there or even close makes them feel inadequate. This is why you must carve your own aspirations in stone, this isn't to say they're original, none are, but they have to be yours and not someone else's.

Speaking Out

You have a voice, as do the vast majority of the near 8 billion human beings on earth. I don't think as a percentage many of them have the true confidence to speak out, say what they'd like or even express themselves. I think people forget that saying nothing is saying something. To not respond is a response. Once you've reread the last sentence, I'll drop in another Mandela quote for this chapter:

> *'Fools multiply when wise men are silent.'*
>
> Nelson Mandela

It pains me to think that so many people do not feel like they have the confidence to say what they want to say. This is different to public speaking, it's one entire feat in itself to muster the confidence to speak in front of people publicly, but the courage required to disagree, to stand for your principles requires genuine courage. It opens doors to scrutiny, to embarrassment and sometimes dislike, but as a by-product of speaking how you feel you can in return find integrity. Integrity is defined as 'the quality of being honest and having strong moral principles'. Your moral principles should be aligned with, if not governed by, your values and it's something I feel is decaying from the world day by day, week by week, month by month.

A Confidence Prefix

It's not always easy to say things or express things, in fact confidence (and lack of) is one of the most common barriers to saying or expressing what we feel. I'll share with you a little hack I use when expressing myself to give myself more confidence when saying it. It will seem really trivial and insignificant, but it's really helped me. So just before I say or express something I'm not confident about, I say, 'I could be wrong.' A friend of mine called Jamie Alderton first taught me this and at the time I had no idea how important it would be when speaking in uncomfortable or new settings where confidence would commonly be lacking.

The idea is to disarm any hostility or wrongdoing with what you're about to say, you're embracing ignorance and even more importantly a potential knowledge gap from the get-go. It's ok to have gaps in your knowledge, we don't get taught enough at school to even know what taxes are. So you can't expect to come out of the education system without ignorance in some forms. For reasons unknown to me, we're not allowed to be wrong at all anymore. You're more likely to be cancelled by culture than get educated by someone. We are so often caught up in our minds about how people may interpret our words when we speak out. Let's say you're in a meeting and you have a suggestion, a better way of doing things, and you don't usually like speaking your thoughts, you don't want to seem like you're discrediting other people's work or being rude with your input. So next time you're in this situation, just precursor your input with 'I could be wrong, but …' I find this is such a simple way to ensure your input isn't taken wrongly; and accepting full responsibility for ignorance and being wrong from the outset can mean such a better received response. People are a lot more accepting of what you say regardless.

> *'As the Island of Knowledge grows,*
> *so do the shores of our ignorance.'*
>
> Marcelo Gleiser, physicist and astronomer

You shouldn't fear ignorance, it's merely a lack of knowledge or information surrounding a subject. We all are on paths of discovery and learning throughout our lives, if you want to say something, say it. If you're not confident about your knowledge in the field, use this precursor to bolster your confidence in what you're about to say.

Worst-case Scenarios

A trait I've noticed very frequently is that self-confident people interpret feedback their own way or from whom they choose to. No matter who you are or what you do, you will get criticism and feedback from it. Even those who make the world a better place get hatred, even tyrants have admirers. There is no person on the planet who wouldn't receive both good and bad critics, both good and bad feedback.

*'Do nothing, say nothing, and be nothing,
and you'll never be criticized.'*

Elbert Hubbard, writer and philosopher

I've often said in social media posts over the years that it is so important to not take criticism from people you wouldn't go to for advice. Could being selective with which criticisms to take to heart be an integral part of the character of the confident? Should you have an ambitious idea that you share with friends and family, even if the majority vote said you could accomplish it, even if the majority thought the idea was great, why is it that the minority of naysayers live rent free in your head? Remember the pessimism bias (page 160)?

When I decided at 24 that I wanted to become a personal trainer, one of my best friends told me that I shouldn't. Now in retrospect becoming a personal trainer and ignoring his advice was one of the single best decisions I have ever made. When I come to think about how I had decided to ignore someone's advice so close to me and try and put my finger on it, was it an abundance of self-belief? Lack of fear? Or could it have to do with the fact I had weighed up logically the real consequences of it all going wrong? I see his point the same way then that I do now. The facts are that most personal trainers don't see their second year out, more than 80 per cent do not survive in the business. People can often overlook the multifaceted nature of being a personal trainer. Although from the outside it can seem you're just training people, you're not. You're a start-up where you are the trainer, the HR manager, the marketeer, the sales team, the online strategy person, the CEO, the COO and in some cases with the receipts you feel like the bloody CFO. You may be the best coach in the world who gets the best results, but if you can't market that then no one will know about how amazing you are and you will go broke.

Looking back now, I definitely didn't sit back and think, 'Yeah, I got this, I can do all of this.' I think it was more leaning towards the implications of it not working out. What were the real consequences, like really, truly and deeply, if it didn't work out? I had worked years in jobs which I didn't particularly have any passion for, nothing to enjoy, and I would like most people dread Sunday nights because I was one sleep away from another 5-day stint of boredom. If I was to shoot my shot at being a personal trainer, if it wasn't the career for me, I could walk away 6–12 months later and go back into what I had done before, not the end of the world, right? Even if I was in a job interview and they asked why I had 6 months in a gym working as a PT, I could just say that I was trying a new career path, hardly unhireable, is it? From a financial standpoint, I had just come back from travelling around South-East Asia spending all my savings, so I was living with my parents. I suppose having them as a safety net was an integral part of having the confidence to go after a completely new career. The courage I had at the time was formed from my relationship to it failing, not to it succeeding, which many people may not have considered before. I didn't jump in with both feet just thinking about success. I was prepared to fail, I had the consequences of what failure looked like in my mind and once I could paint the picture of failure, things didn't seem so daunting.

This is a form of brain exercise required to be practised, I think it's a skill to be honest and I've never forgetten hearing the saying by one of the most influential martial arts coaches of all time:

'All skills are perishable.'

John Danaher

Just because you get good at something, doesn't mean it won't diminish over time. This is why we must at least try to instil some form of practice on a daily basis. I sometimes see confidence like a muscle, it can become well trained and just as easily atrophied. When we see someone effortlessly do 10 chin-ups, we don't see what could easily be years of training that went into being strong enough to pull off that many chin-ups. The best part of this to keep in mind is that practising doesn't mean winning, practising means practising. So, if you are to try something each day to train your 'confidence muscle', it can go wrong and you still can develop for the better. You may aim for 10 chin-ups, but if you only get 5 it doesn't mean you're defeated never to try again. You're that bit closer at 5 than you would be not being able to do any.

When we approach the imaginary chin-up bar, we think to ourselves for a microsecond, 'What if this doesn't work?' Well, in that case there will be no movement across the joints necessary and I will stay hanging here where I am. Perhaps you'll even think about the fact you may just come in short of your usual target; to fail in this instance isn't bad, it's just not getting the desired outcome. It's worth making clear too that not getting the desired outcome is an amazing part of growth and development. If every one of my social media followers bought my personal training programme, I could retire today. No days from a marketing perspective do I even get close to my desired outcome, but I inch closer, that's the real beauty behind running a business. Do enough people apply this to other realms of their life? Not at all.

Public speaking: overcome with fear and the notion that things may not go right. We imagine choking on stage, the light in our eyes and the fear of making a fool out of ourselves. Talking to a stranger: we worry about them rejecting us or not being interested. The idea of a job interview cripples many people from even changing jobs. A job interview on paper is just an interaction with another person, we do these countless times on a daily basis, but in the scenario of a job interview we inflate the importance of it and often can't even be or act like ourselves. In these instances, we struggle to fathom and quantify the outcome of it not working out. Wherever you are, there's no excuse for inaction. Every single person reading this has a higher potential than where they are at now. If you truly didn't think you could do better you would not have bought this book, that's a fact.

Confidence and Anxiety: The Spotlight Effect

When we get down to the nitty-gritty of the many definitions we could muster for what confidence means, we could very easily come to the conclusion that much of confidence is when we can predict success in an outcome. Whether confidence in your sports team, confidence in your partner you just married or confidence in the weather and that it's not going to rain at the time you just booked a tennis court for a knock around tomorrow afternoon. Every time a rugby player kicks for the posts, a football player shoots a penalty or a darts champion throws a bullseye, there must be confidence in the outcome, of predicting success before the attempt. The frustration of missing is the anger of not getting the outcome you've predicted.

To counteract this point, anxiety comes in many forms and has an element of subjectivity between people experiencing it. Whether it's existential anxiety, worrying about something you've said, done or even how something is going to pan out. A question I put to you is this: if you predicted success was the outcome, would you be anxious about it? Probably not. I'm not here with the answers to such a complex topic like anxiety but I am merely alluding to the fact that I feel anxiety can stem from a prediction of something failing. Something not performing, something going badly as opposed to well. So, if we were to create a spectrum with on one side confidence and the other anxiety, we could see confidence as not only a way of doing things that you may not have done before, but as a way to mitigate life's anxiety. Again, I'm not promoting confidence as the antidote to anxiety, but I am saying that if we can action habits that promote confidence and we can see the world through the right lens, we can create an environment that supports one side of the spectrum and moves us further from the other.

Psychologists have investigated the tendency we have to overestimate the amount of attention we're getting at any given point in time. Many people with social anxiety have trouble accepting that the majority of people around them aren't noticing them as much as they may think. Let's say you're late for class one day, you walk in late, everyone's watching, everyone's thinking you're a lazy piece of shit. But in reality, way less people are even taking notice than you'd think.

A psychologist named Tom Gilovich published a paper in 2000 on this exact phenomenon. (See References, p. 263) He randomly assigned one of his students to wear a t-shirt with an embarrassing character on it. The student wearing the t-shirt assumed 50 per cent of people in his class would notice and remember. It turned out to be 25 per cent. His student had massively overestimated by twofold the amount of people who would recall the t-shirt. In the second study, they were to wear a non-embarrassing t-shirt with a famous person on it, like Bob Marley or Martin Luther King Jr. In this second experiment, the student assumed too that 50 per cent of other students would remember the t-shirt. The results for the second test showed that less than 10 per cent of students even realised.

People are quite simply far too busy living their lives and worrying about their own problems, they don't care as much as you think. That's not to be harsh but to remind you that when you do step outside your comfort zones, whether asking for a number or visiting a public gym, although it can feel like everyone is watching your every move, the data shows they're not noticing.

The spotlight effect hits us all on some level and is a massive contributing factor in being self-conscious. You'll never see me in a white t-shirt; the second I put one on, I spill some food I'm eating on the plate and bosh, I'm left with a stain on my white t-shirt. The entire night I'm thinking about this stain on my t-shirt, how embarrassing, but the truth is if the next day I was to ask people I spoke to that evening, very few if anyone would even notice.

'The blemishes and cowlicks that are so noticeable and vexatious to oneself are often lost on all but the most attentive observers.'

Tom Gilovich

Because we live our lives so focused on our actions, appearance and day to day life, we struggle in certain moments to realise other people are not as focused on ourselves as we are. We forget they have the exact internal dialogue going on in their heads that we do in ours, and we don't actually have the capacity to worry equally about other people as we do ourselves.

> 'You wouldn't worry so much about what others think of you if you realized how seldom they do.'
>
> Eleanor Roosevelt

(Seldom means infrequent, not often or rarely. I had to Google it the first time I ever set eyes on the quote.)

So please understand when this bias is taking control of your thought process, you're flooded with the ideas that you may look like a fool or ... STOP. Stop thinking like that, take a deep breath and realise, no one cares even half as much as you think. Even if it does go bad, no one is going to care, no one is going to barely remember and one more attempt at anything makes you more experienced than when you woke up today. Whether in a gym, out for a social occasion or somewhere random, people have enough to worry about for themselves, you should not worry about what everyone else is thinking about you. Be yourself, and do it unapologetically. You can go to bed with one more attempt under the belt than you woke up with; sounds like a win if you ask me.

Declinism

'Declinism is the tendency to see the past in an overly positive light and to view the present or future in an overly negative light, leading us to believe that things are worse than they used to be. Declinism is often a feeling harbored about the overall state of a country, society, or institution, with the view that it is in decline or getting worse.' (See References, p. 263)

This is something I've fallen for even recently. I was watching a film and it was from the 1990s; I thought to myself, wow, how amazing times must have been before smartphones and the internet. Just calling someone, making plans and meeting them there. I thought about the past in an almost utopian sense, I thought briefly that technological advancements since then meant that society and my existence were getting worse, not better, weirdly. So the reason I put this in the book is that it's normal to feel like the present isn't as good as the past, it's been named declinism – this is something we all weirdly manifest. I can't have you closing this book today and thinking the future isn't so bloody good that it's worth changing your habits for, can I? The best days of your life are yet to be had, so diminish any feelings of declinism and appreciate things are getting better, much better. It's just all too easy to slip into the declinism way of thinking time and time again.

'Here's the paradox: the image of a dangerous world has never been broadcast more effectively than it is now, while the world has never been less violent and more safe.'

Hans Rosling, *Factfulness: Ten Reasons We're Wrong About the World – and Why Things Are Better Than You Think*

Contemporary media and social media has tremendously changed the landscape of how news works. Now, rather than being loyal to your paper that you'd get every day by habit, you'll find different media outlets quite literally fighting for your attention via clickbait articles online. News is a thing of the past, traffic is the new currency that is fought for online.

Studies have been done comparing the spread of good news versus bad news to try and understand for a start if the claim of 'bad news travels faster than good news' is true but also to ascertain why humans are more inclined to share, retweet and talk about bad news more so than good news. (See References, p. 263) In the last few years, we've had COVID-19 spoken about daily with new cases, death counts, hospitalisations trending. Variants, vaccine conspiracies, global warming and not to mention severe racial prejudice worldwide, rioting, cancel culture and a general sense of despair shared by so many. I'm convinced that this is rooted to the pessimism bias, a human tendency to expect the worst, but it's important we have confidence in not only our future as a person but the world's future. Looking back nostalgically always paints a more positive picture than in reality, that's why breakups can feel so savage. We only remember the good times, memory serves to remind us of the good while the bad is easily forgotten and buried deep into the subconscious. You can experience declinism first-hand when people say things like 'back in my day it was much better'. But the truth is the world is becoming a better place. Technological advancements in medicine mean more lives are not lost before their time. Poverty, famine and many causes of death continue to decline, and although the numbers are still staggering when reported, they're improving. We're now in a period after the COVID-19 pandemic, and I know people are experiencing declinism within their own minds and I think understanding that it's a perfectly normal human trait made worse by the state of reporting, news and social media. We need confidence in our future, the world's future and our place in it. No self-help book is going to have the answers you need if you think the world is going to shit. You must have optimism instilled into every visualisation you put together in your mind for your future.

GAMBLERS' FALLACY

Have you ever been to a roulette table? You'll see the previous numbers that have come up when the croupier has spun the wheel the last several goes. Have you ever wondered why this is? It's to give you the false sense that what has happened previously will affect the outcome in front of you. If it landed on Red, or Even, that doesn't impact the statistical chances of what is to come.

I want you to think about this not only if or when you gamble, but to not dwell too much on what has happened previous to your opportunity. Odds are odds, previous experiences don't impact the future experiences on a gambling table, even if it does everything in its power to make you feel like it will. Should you go after ambitions in life with the right audacious determination then only your actions are what impacts what happens next, not the previous amount of attempts or outcomes.

The Bystander Effect

The more people that witness something bad happen, the less likely we are to help. I write about this in the book because when this next happens it is your perfect opportunity to use your new-found confidence. Let's say someone falls off their bike right in front of you, absolutely no one else is around, I'm sure you'd say, 'Alright mate, can I help?' But if this was a hugely busy street you'd expect other people to do it and end up doing nothing.

It kind of dispels the idea of safety in numbers: the busier the street, the less likely you would be to get help. When you're in a crowd, it is much easier to pass the responsibility to someone else. It's also known as the 'diffusion of responsibility'. Again, just understanding this is crucial to your future actions. So, why am I bringing this up in a confidence book? Is it to ensure you're the hero the next time something unfortunate happens? Well, yes, but also no. I think the bystander effect plays a role in our inaction. I'll explain. So, when we see someone fall off their bike in the middle of the city after nearly being hit by a bus, we are so sure someone else is going to act that we do nothing. Surely, this must play across to other situations. You see someone in a busy bar that catches your eye, you think about talking to them and saying 'hello' but the bystander effect kicks in. There are so many people around, you expect they must be spoken to by everyone else, surely everyone else sees the same as you, and you freeze expecting other people to do it. Maybe the same as seeing a job opportunity you'd love on LinkedIn, immediately you think, well everyone must be applying for these roles because it's 'such an opportunity'. But what if just like the person on their way to the tarmac on a bike via gravity, the truth is the opposite; where you expect everyone else to be doing it, they're doing nothing. The knowledge of understanding that sometimes the more people you are competing with, the less happens (almost social loafing, see page 106). Where you may assume a popular job or a busy bar would be the worst place for seeking opportunity, it could be your very best. Let's have a commitment between you and I, the next time you witness an apparent bystander effect, do not be the bystander, be the person who enquires, who asks and puts yourself out there. I saw a video on YouTube with actors who lay on the floor ill or pretending to be passed out on the steps of an entrance to a busy train station; dozens of people walked past over stretches of time as long as hours. How much confidence does it really require to step out from the crowd and ask, 'Are you ok?' or 'Can I help at all?' Again, like I said before, when this arises, imagine there's a hidden camera and your parents are watching. What does it really take to see if someone is ok? Before we move to the next chapter, don't promise me, promise yourself. The very next opportunity to be a bystander, be the hero as if your life was a documentary and you're the main character in it.

I attended a personal training business seminar in November 2014. I learned in that seminar how to navigate social media to build a following and eventually one day sell a book off the back of it. There were about 200 people in that room learning the same thing that I did. I do often wonder where those other 199 people are, I don't recall seeing any of their faces on social media. I was no different to anyone else in the room, we all had the same values and the same ambitions, or we wouldn't have paid the money to be in that room. This is probably a great opportunity to remind you of something. Winners and losers have the same goals, the same ambitions, what defines the difference isn't what they aim for, it's what they do and what they don't. Although everyone learns the same content, ideas and actionable tasks, they can all too easily be left not doing any of the tasks because they think, 'Well, everyone else is probably going to do it, what's the point?' I hope if you take one thing from this little segment, it's to never be a bystander in your own life by allowing each opportunity to gain confidence to slip away from you. Be responsible, you have nothing to lose, only to gain, set an example, reap the rewards.

Chapter 8

The Confidence Diet: Values and Behaviours

Our personal values are beliefs that enable our attitudes and our actions. They surround what is important to us, not other people, but us. Our values determine who we want to be, how we want to act and not only how we treat others but how we treat ourselves. We all assign a different amount of importance to certain things in life, for some it's family first, for others they might find money more important. Our actions in daily life usually align with our core values. When looking to make big decisions in life, it's imperative to think about your values.

The Confidence Diet

I do wish I had an actual food plan that spurred on confidence. I wish I could say, 'Oh yes, studies have shown that increasing the amount of carrots in your diet improves confidence by 22 per cent', but I don't. The context of diet in this chapter is going to be different to what you've probably thought before. I want you to think of diet as not only what you put in your mouth, but also what you expose yourself to. Diet is referring to the *kinds of food that a person, animal, or community habitually eats*. Instead, I want you to think about your diet as everything you expose yourself to on a daily, weekly and monthly basis. Where are you when you're using your phone? Who do you 'follow' on social media? What TV do you watch and who do you surround yourself with? Because this is a diet that many people need to alter too. Depending what news network you prefer will change how you see current affairs, your favourite newspaper will change how you see the news. There's a harsh reality that your diet of information is going to influence how you feel about and perceive the outside world. Perception is a big factor in how we feel, we need to really think about that. The same thing can happen to two different people and they can perceive it vastly differently. Let's say 3 people apply for a job, only 1 of them is going to get it, the other 2 get rejected. One could walk away and perceive the rejection as proof that they're not worthy, not good enough or not able to do the job that they applied for. The other person may look at that rejection and think they need to grow, develop, gain experience and apply for a similar job in 6 months when they can work on themselves a little more and bring that to the table when the next opportunity presents itself.

That perception isn't just based on your genetics, it's based on your diet, *not carrots*, the information you expose yourself to and how you process that information. Body confidence is a prime example of this, and unfortunately I do think both ends of the spectrum have gone too far with regards to their standpoints. But think about this: should I have an information diet of male models, physique competitors and many male social media influencers who are on steroids, starved and need to look good quite simply to make a living? That diet isn't going to cause me to be obese, but that diet will cause me to develop a different perception of myself and where I am. I will no doubt feel inadequate, underdeveloped, not to mention many other inferior feelings. Then when presented with the thought of taking my top off when sweating on a long-distance run, I may decide to keep it on due to my perception of how good *I think I look* with my top off. The other end of this spectrum is body confidence gone a bit too far. My controversial standpoint is that it's quite obvious to spot many businesses now employing 'plus size' models to virtue signal their inclusivity quotas. This is a very nuanced debate but at the same time I think that it's fantastic to see more people owning their physique and showing people that it's ok to have stretch marks, cellulite and some body fat. I like to think I've normalised a higher body fat percentage for a lot of men worldwide. I like to remind people all the time that having fat doesn't mean you are fat. If people subscribe to less people in the top 0.1 per cent of physiques and more to people who live a normal life, they'll have a much better perception of what is an acceptable shape to be in to take off a top, or wear a bikini or run in just a sports bra. Again, there is a huge amount of subjectivity to these discussions, but I'm here to remind you that a huge amount of your confidence is governed by *your perceptions*, and your perceptions are governed by *your information diet* that you not only expose yourself to but quite literally subscribe to on a daily basis. The average person is spending 5.5 hours a day on their smartphone. (See References, p. 263) Yes, 5.5 hours! So, when looking to clean up your diet it's imperative you look beyond food. You spend a lot more time digesting information than you do digesting food per day.

Brainwashing may seem quite extreme but don't underestimate the power of information you're exposed to. Look how polarised the world

Screen Time by Generation

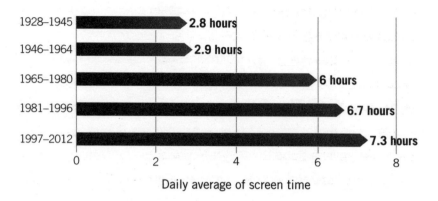

Daily average of screen time

is becoming from conflicting beliefs, values and ideologies. People don't seem to think the media they expose themselves to can impact their perceptions of reality that much, but it really plays a big factor in how you think and perceive things. For a moment, think about the top 10 things or people you subscribe to and ask yourself this: 'Could these things impact my confidence in certain areas?' Then ask yourself: 'Are these benefiting my self-esteem and confidence or potentially hindering it?'

> 'Comparison is the thief of joy.'
>
> Theodore Roosevelt

If it's the thief of joy, don't think for a second it doesn't impact your confidence. For years I've said to my clients to get rid of any pictures they have saved on their phones of other people's physiques. I like to remind them that 'comparison corrodes confidence'. I don't think it's healthy to compare yourself to a stranger. You need to compare yourself to yourself, not other people. Imagine if you took a screenshot of

Elon Musk's net worth and set it as your background, people would think you're bonkers. Don't underestimate the impact of comparison and its impact on how you perceive the world.

Who are You? The Confidence to Be Yourself

Our values play a huge role in who we are and how we act, so it's important to understand the role they play in our actions (and in-actions). If we were to put confidence on one end of the spectrum, the other end would be self-doubt. When faced with self-doubt one of the first places we can look to for support is our own values. Let's say your values are maintaining a high level of integrity and honesty, yet you're feeling like you don't have the confidence to say what you really think, you're jeopardising your important values and that's not a good thing. Say I'm approached by a friend who's not living their best life and they ask me for some advice. I'll first of all ask them what's important for them in life. What do they really want to get from life before the lights go out? What are the essential constituents they need for a good life? I'll get them to say it out loud too. They may say, 'Well, family is the most important thing, it's essential I maintain close contact with them, next would be work-life balance, it's important that I get my work-life right, I want to work to live, not live to work. I also value honesty and positivity, they're two things I'm always wanting to bring to the table.' From there you could ask someone, 'Ok, how well is that being served by your current lifestyle?'

For many it's a harsh reality to see their existence and their values don't add up. I'm a big advocate of letting people know it is not a good deal to live a life you don't enjoy now on the premise you may earn enough money to buy the freedoms you desire later in life. Because if you think there's a magical salary that you'll hit after 5 years of misery where you'll wake up happy, you're potentially – probably – deluded. You need to think about your current values right now. That's not to say they won't change over the coming years, but you need to focus right now and decide what they are, then you need to make changes to your life to ensure you're as close as possible. I have lived a life before where my values did not add up with my actions in daily life, I instead followed the status quo and I ended up feeling what can only be described as suffocated in my own existence. The worst part is, I thought it was normal.

'If you know the operating principles that guide your every action within your day, you know your values.'

This quote's from me. Yeah, me. It seemed a waste to put it within the text, looks much better like this.

Values and Your Self-image: Set Your Own Goals

When you ask yourself the question of who you are, you can reel off your values pretty well as definitions. If there are values you can identify that are negating your self-image and self-esteem, you must identify them and act upon them. For instance, many of you have personal values to look a certain way. That's ok, but to look like someone else as a value, that's not. To be in the same condition as someone who is fit for a living, that's not ok. You don't need to delete or erase values, but sometimes putting them on a slightly different path and trajectory won't only benefit your physiological health, but your mental health too.

Changing Physiology for Confidence

Sometimes there do need to be changes to your physiology. You don't need to have rippling abs, but you need to wear a body you're proud of and that serves you well. Now being proud of your appearance is subjective; you get to decide what winning is, you're the captain of your own ship. If you were to spend the day with some fitness models, I'm sure it wouldn't take long for you to feel like winning needs to be in amazing shape, but you're probably not a fitness model. For instance, for many of my clients I've trained over the years, getting stronger and fitter instilled a sense of pride they thought they'd get simply from losing fat. I also like to say to people that if they knew the car they had now was the last car they'd ever have in their life, they may treat it a little better. That warm bag of bones and muscle you're living in now, well that's not much different. Maybe don't red line it too much and feed it some veggies, sunlight and take a nap now and then when you can.

I'm not saying don't drop unwanted weight, I'm saying there are many other factors than just a mere scale of slim = happiness. Being proud of yourself is a really integral part of being confident, you should be proud that you make your bed in the morning, proud that you get out of bed when your alarm goes off and also be proud that you lift your weights, respect your body and expect a certain demand out of it. This has been an ongoing lesson I've worked on for the last 10 years. There are times periodically that I gain considerable amounts of weight, but rather than pinching fat rolls in front of the mirror I just ask myself some simple questions like, 'How well am I training right now?' or 'Is my performance right now enough to make me feel proud of my physiology?' In most cases, the answer is yes.

So, when eyeballing physiological changes to improve your feeling of self-worth and confidence, make sure you abide by one of my most valuable rules for goal getting: **Choosing the level you win at**. This may seem so trivial but let me explain a little story from the past. Late 2020, a few months into the pandemic, I did a jiu-jitsu tournament and it went terribly. I lost all my matches, I had set very high expectations for it and it crashed down and burned. I did what felt right and went to another tournament a few weeks later and well, I won more matches than I ever have in my life and got a bronze medal. Now, if I was to use the values of a top-level jiu-jitsu athlete they would be very disappointed with bronze, but I am not a top-level athlete, I am a hobbyist that loves it sincerely, but it's important that I don't take on someone else's levels for winning because it skews my ability to set good goals. The bronze medal didn't have to impress anyone but me. All that mattered in the universe was my perception of the win, not anyone else's. If I sat down with you and asked what physiological changes you wanted to make, they can be anything but they have to be your desires. I've sat through hundreds of consultations as a personal trainer and I hear so many people regurgitate what they think I want to hear, or better yet, what someone else has accomplished. People often say, 'I'd like to lose a few pounds.' But I don't believe that for a second. People want their clothes to feel less tight, they want their husbands or wives to want to pounce on them again, they want to be and feel physically fit so they're not worried about an impending heart attack.

If I say a 5 km run is a good goal, to a professional runner that's a warm-up, sure. But if you're not a runner, that can literally be your World Cup final. The subjective nature of goal setting means there are no rules to this game. If it's deadlifting your bodyweight, doing your first set of chin-ups or running your first marathon, whatever it is, if it means a lot to you, no one can take that away from you. If you set sail on making physiological changes to someone else's values and someone else's goals, you're going to have a really tough time sticking to them. In my first tournament, I went in with the mindset, 'I must win, I must get gold.' I didn't realise at the time I was not setting the level I win at, I was using someone else's level they win at to determine mine. Two weeks later I returned thinking, 'I'm going to do my best in every match and enjoy today.' I won more matches than I've ever won at a tournament and I set myself to feel truly happy with what I had accomplished.

A goal has to be personal to you, not anyone else. It may be something as simple as building the courage to train in a gym 3 times a week, it could be about talking in group settings more and it could be about making marginal improvements on how you perform and how you feel; how you look may come later down the line, but it's so important you don't overlook **what winning looks like to you and only you**.

Dopamine

Dopamine is a 'neurotransmitter'. Now I know when you see that word you're going to feel like I'm dropping big words to appear smart. If you remember 'neuroplasticity', you'll remember the breakdown of the meanings. Neuro is related to the nervous system, transmitter alludes to the role of dopamine as a 'signalling molecule'. Dopamine plays a role in how we feel pleasure; it's also known as a 'motivation molecule' that's responsible for 'intrinsic motivation' and our desire to do things. (See References, p. 263)

To quickly recap from my last book *Not A Life Coach*, intrinsic and extrinsic motivation sit differently in our minds, not many people really delve into the differences between them. So imagine things that intrinsically motivate you aren't hard to do because they're rewarding in some way. Walking your dog may be one of your favourite things to do each morning, you're intrinsically rewarded because it makes you (and I hope the dog too) feel good. If you're passionate about a sport, putting your shoes on to go training hardly feels a chore, because you're passionate about it and training for it is personally rewarding to you.

Extrinsic reward is different to this. Extrinsic motivation involves completing a task or exhibiting a behaviour because of outside causes such as avoiding punishment or receiving a reward. So you could say that if you're extrinsically motivated by something, you're doing it to stop something bad happening. For instance, let's say you're working in a job you don't really like, that's extrinsic motivation for money, you're doing it so you don't run out of money (bad outcome) or can't afford your rent (bad outcome). People who coach a sports team for free on the weekend aren't doing it to stop something bad happening, they're doing it because it's personally rewarding and makes them feel good. People that are going to the gym motivated purely by extrinsic motivators probably won't last long, if you're only training to avoid having a heart attack, that's not exactly something that's going to keep fire in your belly long term. If you were to ask someone who trains 3–4 times a week every week why they go to the gym so much, you can bet they'd reply with something along the lines of, 'I really like training, it makes me feel good.' So now hopefully you have a clearer idea of why dopamine can be linked directly with intrinsic motivation, as opposed to extrinsic.

Exercise Rewards and Confidence

I think it's fair to say from the outset that the idea of 'exercising' is subjective. For some, it's their best part of the day, for others, it's their worst part. As we've talked about, motivation is different for different people, so therefore the experience is vastly different. There's an adage that says, 'The only workout you regret is the one you didn't do.' I strongly disagree with this because there are times people need to rest and there are times that people honestly are better off resting. Take it out of context for a bit and there are people who are very productive workers in the workforce, but sometimes you wake up and think you need a day off; no doubt you'll go back to work better charged and feel more inclined to attack the day after a good day off. The way we look at exercise and perceive it in our lives has a massive impact on whether we enjoy it or not. I really dislike the idea of using exercise to burn calories, like you're a hamster on a wheel, that's not how to look at things. Similarly, I don't think you should turn up to work just to earn x per hour. Exercise and training should be seen as an opportunity to get fitter, an opportunity to get stronger, an opportunity to mitigate the likelihood of injury and most important of all, to feel good.

Does exercising really make us feel better? Studies show that physical activity has been shown to be associated with decreased symptoms of depression and anxiety. (See References, p. 263) But again, association is not causation, therefore it's not a general rule of thumb to say,

'Oh you're depressed, just go for a run mate.' It's not an elixir solution for anyone who doesn't feel good. Exercise therapy has become more widely used because of its benefits to the cardiovascular system, emotional state, and systemic functions. (See References, p. 263) I'm not in this chapter at all dismissing medication or the role of psychiatric experts. (Just in case you wondered the difference between psychiatrists and psychologists, psychiatrists can prescribe medication, psychologists can't.) I still believe that these roles are essential and anyone that is dealing with depression, anxiety or even low mood should seek expert advice. At the same time, I just want to bring awareness to the benefits of exercise, and should you reap the benefits from a mental health perspective, the benefits to your physiology that occur at the same time to your cardiovascular system cannot be overlooked. I think it's important that everyone aspires to have a bout of exercise every day, it doesn't have to be too intense or wild, but it just has to give your mind and body the well-needed break it needs from other stressors. Whether escaping the office, the kids or your partner, seeking solace with exercise and training should be at the forefront of ideals for the modern person.

'Oh, you should go do some exercise to de-stress!' That's thrown around a lot too, or to reduce cortisol, which is a 'stress hormone' that gets a bad rap. We need cortisol to get out of bed in the morning so don't hate on it. Exercise I'm afraid is a form of stress too; studies show that moderate to high-intensity exercise provokes increases in circulating cortisol levels. (See References, p. 263) So exercise at a decent intensity is stressful, but we need to understand what physiological and psychological stress really is. It's periods our body is working hard and dealing with things, pretty much. Whether it be challenge or demand, it can feel like tension or fatigue. So from a physiological standpoint, it could be stress from the exercise intensity or how hard you're working, not to mention doing 'too much'.

There is a finite capacity your body can recover from when we look at training. If you go beyond that finite capacity, you'll become fatigued and negate your recovery, mood and hunger for training. It's worth noting that the finite capacity of training that can be recovered from in a week isn't fixed either; if you have poor sleep and/or external influencing factors, your capacity will be shortened, if you have access to better nutrition, sleep etc. you'll no doubt increase that finite capacity.

So doing more than your body can recover from will start to deteriorate your results and become counterintuitive to the original goal or aspiration. Moving on to psychological stress, this can be sneakier than people even realise, even things that can seem as trivial as notifications on your phone, these pop up, 'boing', and cortisol levels spike. I've had my mobile phone on 'do not disturb' mode for the best part of three years now. Studies show smartphone push notifications produce a decline in task performance and negative effects were shown during smartphone overuse when researching psychological or physical characteristics. (See References, p. 263) Mental and physical stress are different but exist within the same central nervous system, so they're held to be coexisting irrespective of having different causative mechanisms.

The reason I turn this into a bit of a science lesson is because it's important we don't hold exercise up just as a way to 'de-stress'. Stress management is a whole entirely different field but it is imperative to associate exercise with feeling good. I know most fitness blogs that have existed in the last 20 years throw around the idea of 'endorphins'.

'Oh, you must exercise to get a hit of endorphins, you'll feel amazing'. Endorphins are chemicals produced by the body to relieve stress and pain. (See References, p. 263) Endorphins are released during painful experiences, such as when you sprain your ankle, to temporarily relieve pain and discomfort. They're also released during pleasurable moments, such as eating hedonic foods like chocolate, having sex, or most commonly attributed to exercising. (See References, p. 263)

I don't want this conversation to go too much into the hormonal impacts of exercising to be honest, I didn't want my third book to be called *Not An Endocrinologist*. The reason is that although I can appear to look very smart and what not, discussing these complex words and going into the scientific debate can cause everyone to gloss over. 'Hi, my name is James and not to get too complex but there's these protein chains called Peptides'. No, that's not what this book is about. Instead, I want to draw on my own personal experiences in feeling good and exercising and why I believe we 'feel good' from training and why I think the real reason people came back to use me as their trainer thousands of times. Before I get into that, I need to distinguish two common terms and break them down a bit.

Progressive Overload in Confidence: Training versus Exercising

For many people reading this, they'd think these two things are the same, but to me, they're not. Two people can run on a treadmill, but for these two people, although doing the same exercise, they are not doing it with the same intentions, and intentions are incredibly important when distinguishing the difference between someone who is exercising and someone who is training. I'll make clear that in this chapter and in my life's work, it has never been to deter someone from exercising, not at all, if anything the opposite. At any point in time, a person burns a certain amount of energy per minute, let's say, just like a car in traffic ticking over; the size of the car and the size of the engine is going to correlate with the fuel usage, even at rest. This is the same with people, the bigger the person the bigger the requirements. Now, should you get this person to work harder, rev harder when driving so to speak, you increase the requirements of that person. So it's incredibly easy to get people to exercise, you just need to get them to rev their engines, right? I've said for years, it's very easy to make someone tired, it's not so easy to train someone. Any person can go to a boot-camp and be instructed to do as many burpees as they can in a minute, this would fatigue even the fittest of people. But this is exercising someone, you're just revving their engine. Progressive overload is like revving to the optimal amount, then taking your foot off the accelerator and selecting the higher gear and repeating. Many of the world's personal trainers are guilty of just this, exercising people and hiding it under the guise of proper training. When you follow someone's YouTube workout, that's exercising. I'm not making this a bad thing either, it's just a dose of reality that all you're doing is burning more calories than at rest and probably leaving a rather sweaty mess in your front room.

Training is different because of one integral part of the entire thing, one thing that I think is an unappreciated key component of not only becoming fitter, stronger but also becoming happier and more confident as a by-product. For an exercise to be transformed into 'training' it must encompass progressive overload. Progressive overload is when we aim for small progressive, trackable, measurable developments in a skill over time. Every book I've written says 'what gets measured gets improved' and the majority of people exercising are not measuring anything to score progression over time. When we look at successful businesses, data is so important, so you have visibility over what is working and what doesn't. Some people won't agree with this, but I believe data motivates people to do more. Look at what smartwatches and Strava have done for runners. 'Well done, that was your fastest 5k.' Giving people real-time data on their performance revolutionised the average hobbyist to push their limits. Google analytics enabled people online to realise where their traffic was coming from to their websites to double down their efforts on what was working and to reduce resources to what wasn't.

Psychological changes cannot be physically seen, measured or quantified. I said about my last book *Not A Life Coach* that it was a hugely exciting project for me to write a book where someone could change an incredible amount of times over 6–12 months but their DEXA (bone density) scan wouldn't change, their bone mass, muscle mass, etc. would remain the same but they'd become a completely different person.

A lot of physiological changes are not visible for a long time. Fat loss takes time, muscle growth takes time, but strength increases happen a lot faster than you'd realise. When a sales team performs well, they're told about it and incentivised; when someone runs a personal best, they're told about it as they finish the workout. When someone personal bests in a CrossFit gym, the coach congratulates them. So many people in the world think they're built differently, into a dichotomy of 'loves exercise' and 'hates exercise', when the reality is closer to the fact that so many people are exercising to make themselves tired and the rest of the world are training towards a goal that they can progress in. They're progressively overloading what they can in every aspect of their life. This is why I often disregard the narrative that you should exercise to get endorphins or to 'feel good'. Instead, you need to train to seek progression in your life, it doesn't fucking matter where you start. It matters where you are going, where the next step is and where the next inch is. I am an honest believer that the true happiness from training comes from clawing those small margins and then cherishing the moment for a small fraction of time before setting the next goal. A good coach doesn't just show you that you're stronger, they're proving that what you're doing is working and giving you a reason to continue. You're no longer a hamster on a wheel trying to make yourself tired, you're someone on a ladder, with nothing in your ambitions bar the next step. Whether a squat, a chin-up, a muscle-up or a 5 km personal best, human beings have a 'fire in the belly' for goals, tangible goals that they can hit. True pleasure comes from not just the pain that comes with training hard but the belief that the pain was worth it, that the pain is worth it. That's the difference between training and exercising.

What about failing? So glad you asked. People who exercise often have a goal that exists outside of progressively overloading. It can be a weight, a look, a desire or usually a utopian ideal that they'll get to a certain look, be content with their reflection and live happier ever after. This rarely is the case, I assure you. When you exist within the realm of seeking progressive overload you do not exist in a split between 'I'm not there' versus 'I am there' which can often be translated into 'I am unhappy' versus 'I'm happy'. Trust me, I was here for years when I became a personal trainer, I didn't think anyone would respect me or take me seriously unless I was chiselled, muscular and had the body of a Greek god. I improved my physique so much over so long and never found happiness because I was never 'I'm there' so I remained 'I'm unhappy.' As a by-product, I never felt confident in how I looked which resulted in not feeling confident in who I was. They're tied together closer than most people even realise or think. When I changed into someone who sought progressive overload, I didn't have a change of goals per se, I had a change in values and what I valued. This is massive, I wish I could write this chapter 10 times. Like I said before about the two people running on the treadmill, one exercising, one training. There is a distinction in their values, what they are aiming for is governed by what they deem is important: looking a certain way versus the next measurable goal I can accomplish.

*'Progressively overloading means there is no end point,
there is no finish line, there is only the next step. The
dangers of aiming for a goal is that you hit that goal and
have no idea what to do next.'*

James Smith

With training, there is no finish line, there is no finished product, there is only the next metric, whether time, whether weight, you only have a blinkered approach to progress, not to finishing. Bestselling author and psychologist Carol Dweck couldn't say anything more true than, 'Becoming is better than being', right? So why is there so much impor-tance in progressing? Because when you're continually progressing and developing you get a sense you're on the right path, and that is one of the most fulfilling emotions to behold. When you continually get stronger you realise, 'If this wasn't what I wanted, I wouldn't be here getting stronger.' If it's getting fitter and your times are improving, you can stand back and think, 'If I didn't want to get fitter, I wouldn't have improved my times so often.' Remember, as I said before, passion can often be a result of your efforts, you're often not fully sure what you believe in until you've done it. When you're progressing and moving forward with your objectives, it's hard to give focus to confidence and the lack of that may lurk in the back of your mind. Do you think businesses that are profitable are worrying about their confidence? No. Because what they're doing is working and they're still doing it. Having something work for you and you see that it's working, to recognise it at every victory you cherish progressing, is what ultimately gives you confidence in not only what you're doing, but the why behind why you're doing it.

Interrogative self-talk

I don't believe that people are scared of gyms or that they lack the confidence to be in there. I believe a lot of the time they're yet to prove to themselves why they're doing it, they're yet to see the proof in the pudding and they're yet to experience what it feels like to become obsessed with the next step on their ladder. People care about what others think of them so much because they don't care enough about what they're doing. Someone turning up to the gym or an event to progress has a mind occupied with winning, not what other people are doing. Should you feel the last few weeks of squatting your max got a little easier and you decide to put an extra 2.5 kg on each side of the bar for this week, that look in the mirror into your own eyes is about saying to yourself, 'I've got this.' You're on the precipice of having a new set of goals once you finish your sets. There is no sweeter feeling.

The beauty of failing is this: should you bite off more than you can chew and you get to your last set of exercise and it's too much, you don't get past the precipice. Instead of your exercising mindset thinking, 'I am not there', the training mindset thinks, 'What can I do to get there?' This is interrogative self-talk.

Say you're posed with something that's really challenging to you: public speaking, asking a stranger something or even more trivial than that. Are you better off *telling* yourself you can do it or *asking* yourself? Studies have shown that interrogative self-talk produces better task performance than declarative ones. (See References, p. 263) Many gurus over the years have proclaimed that you can assure yourself easily by doing something cheesy and speaking to your own reflection in the mirror and saying, 'I can do this' or 'I deserve this'. However, psychologists over the years have been fascinated by the idea of rather than telling yourself you can do something, to ask yourself. This is a form of actually getting your brain to work on the outcome rather than just assuming it. Thinking about what can go wrong is better than trying to tell yourself nothing can go wrong. So, when you challenge yourself with a question, you can create answers that break down your fear of doing it in the first place. It's not manifestation, it's more so the idea of saying things to yourself so they form some type of existence. It seems that rather than 'pumping' yourself up for a task or event, you may be better off 'asking' yourself up.

'Can I really speak at my office meeting tomorrow on that task that's been keeping me awake? Well, yes, because I delivered a good talk last week, I got great feedback. Am I capable of slowing down the words and presenting it in a slightly more confident way? Well, I do have more experience since I presented for 20 minutes last week. Can I make this the best talk I have ever presented at work? Well, this is the perfect opportunity for me out of all the talks I've done before. Now that I think about it, this is not something to worry about, instead this is a perfect opportunity for me to show my colleagues what I am capable of.'

Interrogative Self-Talk in action: don't tell yourself, ask yourself, then answer yourself.

So as you can see, training versus exercising is a bigger example of mindset than it is work rate in the gym. It's not only a way of seeing problems, it's a way of dealing with them. Human beings for hundreds of thousands of years have been problem solvers, it's what we do.

Training and Confidence

This is a multifaceted element of the confidence topic. I've spoken about the direction of what you're training for breeds confidence, similar to passion being a result of believing in what you do and having it tied to your core values. Confidence isn't too dissimilar. When you train and seek progressive overload, you're finding out two crucial things with parallels to everyday life:

► You find out where you are; it doesn't matter where you start. So many people lose so much mental energy so focused on where they start, that they lose sight of where they are going or where they could end up. Stripping your ego, avoiding distractions and taking note where you are is the first and very important step. Whether being a start-up business with no assets or income or being someone returning from a 6-month break from training, the first step is exactly that, to determine where the first step is. It doesn't matter if you've lost strength or lost fitness, it matters that you take note of where you are so you can do one simple thing and one thing only, progress forwards, look at the next rung on the ladder, nothing else.

▸ You identify what is next, where is next and how to get there. You need a plan of action. The best part of this is: it doesn't need to be perfect, it just needs to work. I mean, in this book from first page to last, I assume there will be a couple of grammar mistakes. I'm only human after all. That shouldn't be the focus, the book will either empower you or it won't. The training plan will either make you fitter or stronger, or it won't. Life is about investing energy, time and effort into things that work. Not to find something that's perfect. I've often spoken about life having so many things on a spectrum, from 'sub optimal' to 'optimal'. If we can make a process more optimal, by going to sleep earlier, eating more vegetables or periodising our workout better, we do it. If we can't, that's fine, it's not failing, it's just sub optimal. Sinking 3–4 beers each weekend isn't optimal for a lot of reasons, but for balance and living a life it's pretty necessary for a lot of people. Instead of looking back on your life and asking, 'Is this perfect enough?' we should look at it and say, 'Is this working?'

When things are working, when they are progressing this produces confidence as a by-product. Even to people who criticise your work, your workout regime, whatever it is. If you know it's working for you, you'll develop the ability to let their criticisms slide like water off a duck's back.

The second part of the confidence and training paradigm is that well-trained people feel better about themselves. Meta-analysis (a study of studies) data shows that children experience positive short-term effects on self-esteem from exercising. Although self-esteem is more to do with how you appreciate and value yourself, whereas confidence is more to do with your belief in your abilities, there is a tremendous overlap between them both. I don't think we can only make one side of the argument here and say, 'Ok, fitness makes you feel better.' We need to look at the counterpart of why neglecting your health and wellbeing could all too easily open the door to confidence destruction. There are countless reasons why someone may not be in their best bit of health. I wrote my first book, *Not A Diet Book* to make clear how dieting works, to eradicate a lot of the nonsense that exists in the diet industry and give people the tools to change. In my second book, *Not A Life Coach* I made clear to people that fulfillment and values are imperative for success and the importance of having a work life and personal life that feels personally rewarding will make everything easier. In some respects, the second book was a precursor to the first. You need to get your life right before you make changes to it, or you may find it hard to stick to. As someone who grew up pretty overweight, I understand first-hand what being overweight does to confidence. I know what it's like to constantly pull your shirt down when you stand up in case a bit of it gets stuck in your rolls of fat. I know what it's like when people make fun of you when you're eating your lunch and I know the destructive things it can do to your confidence, from asking someone out to not being picked for any sports team. I spent the majority of my childhood being picked last in physical education classes. This will give you a fairly accurate insight as to why I have a chip on my shoulder large enough to want to flip the world over as to how we see and deal with weight loss.

Not being fit makes us question our confidence in how healthy we are. Not being as slim as we'd like makes us question how much we're respecting ourselves. Not pushing ourselves towards any tangible goals makes us feel like we've given up on pursuing better and that we're some type of failure because of it. I think it's not wise to assume that being in good shape automatically means you're confident, because I don't think that's true. Some insecurities will follow you irrespective of the physical condition that you're in. But working towards something and knowing you're on the right path when it comes to all things fitness and outside, generates a sense of wellbeing and contentment. Knowing you're becoming better really helps you accept where you are, because you know this isn't it, this is just where you're at now, you're too busy dwelling on the next step to worry about where you currently are. I think your biggest worry within training should be stagnation; as long as you're progressing in the right direction, that's all that should matter.

Values and Decision Making

Being confident in the decision you're making comes from aligning it with your values. 'Am I sure I want to do this?' 'YES, because it's in line with my values.' One example that I think many of us consider might be that you're staring down the barrel of a pay-cut to go to a job you would actually enjoy. I was faced with this decision when I became a personal trainer at 24. I asked myself if it was the right decision. Now if my values were just about money, the answer would have been no. However, my values are more about freedom, work-life balance and not hating Mondays. So I made the decision with full confidence and in hindsight it was leaning on my understanding of values that enabled me to make one of the best decisions I have made in my life so far.

I have always liked to differentiate pleasure and happiness as two separate things. Pleasure can be found in short hits anywhere: some fast food, a bit of cake, getting drunk with your friends or a night on the town. True happiness comes from aligning your actions with your values, waking up on Christmas day with your family, it's the time you spend with your dog and it's witnessing a sunset on holiday. I personally experience the difference when it comes to gifting. If I buy myself something expensive, it's for pleasure. However, if I buy something expensive or ludicrous for someone else, it gives me happiness. I don't believe anyone's values align with buying something from Gucci or getting pissed on a night out, but I do think people's values can align with setting an early alarm to watch the sun come up or to get a dog and give it the best life possible.

What am I getting at? I'm saying that we lean on our values to enable us to make the best decisions possible; confidence is out of the equation really, if you think about it. When faced with a crossroads of how to act we must know exactly what we cherish and make a decision based on that. You don't always need more confidence to decide on whether to leave your job, you need to lean on your values and decide what is ultimately going to make you happier. You need to distinguish that it is happiness and not pleasure you'll elicit from the decision. Once you're sure that the decision is in your best interest for your identity and the values tied to it, you don't need to look for more information or to spend more time thinking, you know what needs to be done and you do it. Once you know your decision will be right for your values, you won't need confidence, because you know it's the right thing to do. There may be some readers now in a long-term relationship or marriage, and I'm here as a 30-something guy without a family giving you advice. Your decision to be with this person may have been absolutely right for your values when you did it, but people change, situations change and as we need and want different things in life, sometimes we need to act on ensuring our actions remain in line with our values. That doesn't make it easy, but it sometimes makes it right. It's not more confidence you need here, it's clarity, and that clarity comes from looking at what you want from your life then asking yourself if your current set-up is delivering on those wants.

Passion Reinvented

I don't say this often, but I may have been wrong. What do I mean? Well, I've said openly many times before to 'find your passion' and I think I may be wording it a little wrong in some contexts. Passion is not on the landscape, it's not out there, you won't stumble across it one day by accident. Passion comes as a result of doing things you believe in, it comes as a by-product of doing things you value and doing things that align with your values. Simon Sinek, one of my favourite authors, cleverly aligns passion with profit. I don't think it's a good idea to merely start a business to profit and make money, many people do, but I don't think that's passion, that's just money, right?

What I mean is, you do something that aligns with your personal values, and at first it feels right. You wake up out of bed knowing you're doing what feels rewarding to you. For me this was personal training, I know it can seem like merely rep counting to so many people, but my pain points earlier in life with my physique, how I felt about myself and the insecurities that came from it, meant that when I became a personal trainer I wasn't passionate about it. How could I be? I was too busy being an imposter on my first day to be passionate. Think about it, any person who's truly passionate now wasn't when they started; when they started it was their values that led them to knowing it was right. When you work in an environment that aligns with your values, passion is the by-product, not the way in, but the way out. It was only when I spent days, weeks and months working within a field I truly believed in that I realised I was not just fuelled by coffee and leftovers from dinner in Tupperware, but passion, something deeper in the belly, something that made me want to fight every inch to reach more people and impact more lives.

Say you see a market for something innovative that helps people, I mean truly helps them. You'll get into that business because you believe it can help someone and your values no doubt align with help-ing people. You then remain invested in that business, the early mornings, late nights and so forth, because you believe strongly that the outcome will align with your personal values, right? Five years later, you've not felt like any of it was truly work. Why? Because passion in many respects is believing that what you're doing aligns with your personal values. This isn't a business book, but when I do take business talks I always remind people, should you do something you enjoy and find rewarding, the profit comes as a result; you invest into the machine of doing something you believe in. If you have a blinkered approach to doing what aligns with your values, the profit and the passion come later.

To conclude, if you're yet to find your passion in life, that's normal, there are probably a few billion people feeling the same, waiting for it to come along and hit them in the face. Little do many know that perhaps instead of seeking passion, seek investing yourself into something that aligns with your values, then look for passion as a by-product later, not a precursor that comes before.

Values and Behaviours

Left on autopilot, human beings can be destructive. If you don't believe me, look at when we start to drink, our values diminish and disintegrate. Your core values in your work and even sometimes relationships go out the window. Drinking can be self-destructive, not going home or turning up to work can be self-destructive and making bad decisions and being lured into debauchery is often self-destructive. Drunk people can tell you rationally the implications of doing things, they just care less when drunk about the implications of it. That's not to paint alcohol in just a negative light, it can be constructive, acting as a social lubricant to create the ultimate setting for first dates, business dinners on the expenses and even to rekindle date nights for those further down the line in a relationship. It's just to bring to your attention that your behaviours are hugely influenced by your values. If you look at anyone who has stopped drinking, chances are it's because their actions were conflicting with their values and it made them feel like shit. Personally, I drink a lot less these days because it clashes with my values for being productive, for being active and for feeling good about myself. I need to establish that if or when I am invited for beers, it's to fill my quota of happiness through the values I cherish for being there for my friends and to talk to them about their lives, ups and downs. I need to ensure that I'm not looking to fill my quota of a quick hit of pleasure under the guise of being a good friend. If you want to stop drinking, you need to ensure you can find something that you like and enjoy more than drinking, and that's the tough part for so many people.

Human beings can be vastly self-destructive too, look at an affair or merely being unfaithful. Is throwing a marriage down the drain for one sexual encounter really a good deal? Not really, but it happens. Is feeling hungover and feeling anxious about your behaviour from the night before really a good deal? Not really, but it happens, for many, most weekends. I think that people becoming in tune with their values is integral for better decisions to be made in their life. Look at people who turn to religion, it's not so that a man in the sky looks after them. It's so that they can have some clarity to the values they should cherish and then act a certain way afterwards. As I've grown older, I've come to appreciate religion and different belief systems more and more, because you simply know they're about instilling strong values in people so they behave in a certain manner. Although there are extremist groups out there painting certain religions in a bad light, we know that there are millions if not billions of people who live life being better humans based on the values and behaviours learned from their religions.

If you drink too much, you don't just need to stop drinking and that will be the end of it. You need to lean on your values and ask yourself what behaviours and actions, and crucially, consequences, are more in line with them. Do you cherish feeling good, do you cherish being productive on a Sunday? If so, there could be happiness to be found in choosing a path closer to your values, and less to what will bring you a temporary high. Find that thing, person or activity you like more, then try to do that instead.

The point I am getting at throughout this entire part of the book is where sometimes you have seen others act in certain ways and seen their actions pertain to a level of confidence in the way they act, they answer and they do things. It's important we don't just assume they are more confident than you in life and perhaps that they are just better clued up with exactly what their values are and that when your values of you and your identity are at the forefront of your mind, acting and responding is no longer such a thing to be worried about. Perhaps those people you think are 'naturally' confident are actually just very well understanding of their values.

Insecurities and Confidence

Want to know what other self-destructive behaviour many people elicit on a daily basis? Insecurities. Internal projections of thoughts and feelings, many times not backed up by fact. There are two types of people in my eyes, those who admit to having insecurities, and liars. I think insecurities are normal, but if you do not control them and break them down, they will affect your life, and rarely in a positive way. Negativity bias (see page 75) coupled with insecurities can really dampen the vitality of your soul.

Insecure (adjective): (of a person) not confident or assured; uncertain and anxious.

Insecurities are a feeling of being inadequate and include a level of uncertainty. Now I find that insecurities exist in the exact same places that we find issues with confidence; relationships, professional lives and the fastest growing realm I expect would be physiological insecurities. The way our perceptions and emotions are intertwined with social media, television and printed media, it's all too easy to get caught up with the top achievers in whatever field, whether financial, fame or fitness. Being surrounded by people in incredible shape is going to make you feel more insecure about your physique and physiology. In some of my fitness talks over the years, I've said that if you were to compare your physique and abilities to that of your whole town you probably wouldn't be too far from the top. If you're a gym go-er, you're in the top tier of people within the UK for a start already.

243

(See References, p. 263) It's estimated that just over 10 million people have gym memberships in the UK, out of a total population of 68.4 million people. (See References, p. 263) That's only 15 per cent of the population with a gym membership, so if you're using yours, even just once a week, you're in the top 15 per cent of people already. It doesn't feel that way though, huh? If there was a genetic trait that 1 out of 1,000,000 people had which meant they literally didn't do anything each day and had the physique of a Greek god, you'd have 68 people to follow on social media and that's just the UK alone. This is where I feel social media really can skew our realities of what normal is and therefore leave us with a sense of inadequacies.

So, where do we start with our inadequacies and our insecurities? To begin with, take note of them. If you have faults, whether physical, intellectual or social and it's causing you to feel inferior because of that, well that's normal. It's normal to feel that way and to want to improve yourself. But the problem lies where some people feel so bad about themselves and their flaws and faults that they're unable to take any action. It's almost like you're frozen and unable to take the first step to bettering your position. If you're not reaching your full potential or if you're not the best version of yourself possible, that's not a reason to take things so personally that you're frozen and unable to progress. Because no one is really the best version of themselves, we all have flaws and that's not a bad thing, it's a big part of living as a human being. If you take your inadequacies too personally and too much to heart, you won't be able to progress. When we criticise ourselves and put ourselves down, there is no one to adjudicate the internal dialogue and to identify where many of us are far too harsh on ourselves.

For me, the solution to many of these emotions is to simply *work on your weaknesses*. If you haven't taken time to identify them, you really need to think about them. If I look at my childhood, I was bullied for being overweight, I was made to spend the majority of my time growing up feeling inadequate and self-conscious to a degree. I still remember the names of every boy in my primary school and I still know exactly what they called me, but it took about 20 years for me to realise how much of a favour they've actually done me. It was identifying my weaknesses and working on them tirelessly that eventually put me in a position to teach people exactly what I didn't know as a child. Again, with jiu-jitsu, I recall a moment having a bit of a playfight with a friend on a beach; I felt powerless, clueless and unable to think about what to do next. It was that feeling of being powerless that lit the inner desire to work on the weakness. I emailed an instructor of a local Brazilian jiu-jitsu gym and that was that. I got my white belt and wore my first ever Gi (which is the martial arts equivalent of a dressing gown.)

Over the years I now see these painful emotions of inadequacies and insecurities as paths which we can take. Could so many of these emotions be down to the fact you don't yet see them as pathways to progress and instead as hurdles you can't fathom climbing over? This takes a certain attitude, a certain ethos and a very honest dialogue with yourself as to what really lies deep down in your mind about what you're insecure about and the inadequacies you feel. And I hope that what we covered in Part One has already started to help to change and strengthen that mindset.

People often ponder the meaning of life. I do a lot and bloody hell, I'm not even close to having an answer. But in some respects, what better way to live your life than to keep busy working on your weaknesses? It's certainly a more productive means of overcoming an existential crisis. This doesn't mean going after every weakness you have and becoming a master: I can't do double-unders on a skipping rope, I can barely do single-unders and I'm happy for my life to go on like that. But when it came to being an overweight kid who was hugely criticised for the way I looked, when it came to being a man who felt inferior on the beach that day, those were things I didn't want to go through life without addressing. I'm not ever intending to compete in CrossFit so the weakness of skipping was never an issue. But when my goals in life are to feel good, I needed to do the work to feel and look better. I've always idealised the idea of looking after whoever I'm with, whether a partner, a friend and one day a father to children of my own, so the goal of being able to handle myself was what set me on the path of working on a weakness that stood between where I was and where I want to be in life.

Goal switching can be a dangerous game, because some people will just create a new ruleset and they can bypass all the hard work. For instance, instead of transforming themselves to getting fit and healthier they may just create a distraction goal to bypass the hard work. They may swap the goal for just going to the gym a minimum of twice per week. Although still a goal, they've changed the goal so that the required work is reduced. Goal changing on the other hand can be an incredible benefit to your situation. You may be hugely insecure about your level of fitness, worried that you may have a heart attack throwing a frisbee with your dog or child. You then might enrol in a Couch to 5k, then suddenly you're eyeing up a 10k run. Before long you want to do your 21k half-marathon stint. In this case, always upping the ante on your goals is only going to benefit your position, but always take note when the goal is shifted to avoid doing the work.

There is pain to be found in pursuing a difficult goal, the pathway to improving weaknesses isn't an easy one. Sometimes that pain and failure along the way is essential on the road to transforming who you are. Losing can be a great motivator and winning can make people weak. So, let's say you're insecure about the way you look, let's say you feel inadequate from a physiological perspective, you're unfit and haven't been to the gym in a very long time. You must ask yourself: can I work on this? Can I improve where I am at? That improvement can be any way, shape or form you like it to be.

Now I want you to stop and ask yourself the following questions:

- ▶ Is there anything I can do right now to work on my feelings of being insecure?
- ▶ What actions can I implement in my daily life to feel less inadequate?
- ▶ What is something I can do on a weekly basis to better the position I am in right now?

These changes don't have to be massive, added up they can have huge differences. For instance, in jiu-jitsu you get a stripe to show progress, 4 stripes and you're soon to get your next belt promotion. Setting a goal of getting a black belt is huge, it's 10 years of commitment, but setting a goal of getting a stripe? That's 6 months of hard work. On a smaller scale, that's just saying I'll attend class three times a week. When looking at weight loss, it's the same. Small goals. If you wish to lose 1 lb of body weight you'd want to set small goals like hitting a step count, a daily calorie target and going to the gym three times per week. Think of it as the below:

- Identification of insecurities and inadequacies. Write each one down.
- What can be done to action each one?
- Implementing behaviour to change each one? How does it look?
- Small and large-scale changes achieved over time. What does this look like on a weekly basis? What does it look like on a monthly basis?

And the positive outcome of having insecurities to begin with motivates change. I see it like this:

A goal that pushes you + a requirement for self-transformation = maximum motivation

The Confidence-humility Connection

Like most things in life, balance is of the utmost importance. Take a look at the diagram opposite and imagine you're beginning a journey from the bottom left to the top right. Because whether you know it or not, you are. Whether it be your professional life, a new hobby or a new sport. You must steer towards improving competence, with confidence coming as a natural duality. We must ensure we do not steer too far to the left or right. Too far right and we're feeling like an imposter,

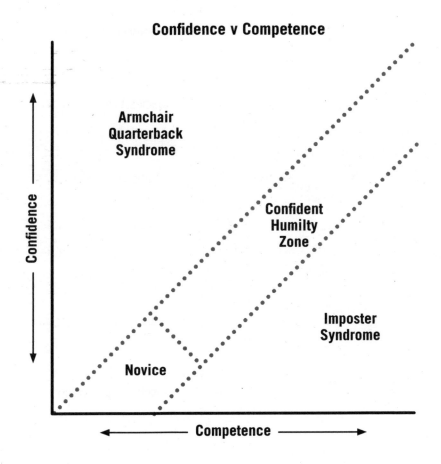

perhaps slightly out of our depth, too far to the left and we're facing arrogance and being 'overconfident'. Like a ship at sea with a captain behind the wheel, it's not a straight direction but many adjustments to the wheel over time that allow us to remain on course and find the perfect balance between humility and confidence.

Finding balance isn't as easy as it sounds and when researching this topic, I looked into whether finding this balance was harder for women than for men. I found it fascinating to find out that women have less confidence in their own performance and more faith in a group's

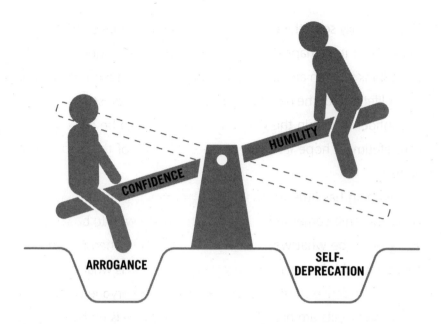

performance, whereas men are the opposite, being confident in their own performance more than a groups' performance. (See References, p. 263) This doesn't necessarily point to the fact that 'men are more confident than women' which many blogs online point to. When following the trails of evidence, many people theorise that the differentiation between gender when looking to overconfidence in performance is due to human evolution and the direct nature of competition between men vs men competing, rather than women who would compete perhaps in more subtle and indirect manners. (See References, p. 263)

I'm not coming at this argument from a side either; I'm not saying that being either gender is an advantage or disadvantage here, if anything you could find benefits and hindrances of either male or female. When looking at men and women across populations, we can say with confidence that men are taller than women on average.

That's actually something that can't be changed or influenced if you think about it. Perhaps if we began manipulating genes, sure. But I don't think women are going to become taller than men on average in our lifetimes or the next generation. But I hope you see the beauty of confidence within this context: confidence *can* be influenced in your lifetime. I hope it's influenced by the end of this book to be honest.

A woman has little to no control over whether or not she is an 'outlier' when it comes to her height, should she wish to be tall. But if you wish to be what we could deem an 'outlier' when it comes to confidence, this is very much in your control. This is what makes the trait of confidence so unique – it's available to everyone whereas so many other traits are not. What I'm saying is there is no book in the world that you can put down and set out actionable progressions to become taller, but with this book and the understanding of so many topics I've discussed, I think it's brilliant that you can close the final page and decide on how you're going to react in certain situations in the future compared to how you may have acted them out in the past: that is, to become more confident.

Accomplishments

'Sooner or later, those who win are
those who think they can.'

Paul Tournier, physician and author

One of the currencies of confidence is accomplishments. This is where it's imperative to ensure your objectives are accomplishable right from the start. I don't want you to think, 'Ok, tomorrow I will be confident when I wake up.' Instead, I want you to ask yourself, 'What can I accomplish tomorrow in my quest for a more confident life?' When we see the word 'accomplishments' it's all too easy to think that this would mean something of substantial significance that would mean you getting a trophy to put in a cabinet at home, but this isn't the case. There are accomplishments like winning a tournament, a prize at work or even a badge of honour, but they don't have to be such grandiose feats. As I mentioned earlier in the book, you need to find a level of courage you currently have in order to accomplish the next step. For instance, applying for a new job or even the thought of interviewing for something you have little experience in, can seem very daunting, right? But what about the idea of just updating your CV? Surely every person has the courage to do that? So you do that. Then what? Well, what's next, sending it to an employer, what is really to lose from doing that? Let's use jiu-jitsu again as a hot topic. I've been asked at least a thousand times, 'James, how do I get into jiu-jitsu? I want to give it a go, but I'm really scared.' I say to them to just Google the local gym, that's it. I'm not asking you to compete or fight someone, just to Google it. When you know the name of the gym that's cool, think about it for a bit then seek the next step, make contact. Then arrange to go in and look around, any fitness/martial arts business would love to have someone look around and see if it's a fit for them. Then what? A trial or taster session. At any point you can leave the quest for small accomplishments, at any point you can step off the ladder. If you went to visit a gym and you don't think it's for you, that is fine – yet so many people never even make it to that point because they use their lack of confidence as a barrier to entry.

The biggest buildings in the world are built one level at a time; each level is of the utmost importance as it supports the next. I know it can seem so daunting to erect what can feel like a skyscraper, but at the outset your focus should never be on the top, it should be at the next level and so forth. Every level is a small accomplishment in your ambition, and over time you'll accrue self-esteem and confidence like you would points when using a credit card on purchases. You won't even realise that it's there until you're in a position to use it.

Conclusion

The Past

Much of who you are today is based on who you have been and what happened to you throughout your life to this very moment right now. This isn't my way of lying you down on the sofa and pretending to be your therapist, this is me telling you how you have come to be here right now coming to the end of my book. We can't dwell on the past, but we can appreciate it. We must leverage our past to create positive actions for the future, not to use our pasts as a reason to dwell on things or remain unhappy in certain situations.

I often reflect on the impact that being adopted has had on me. There are not enough pages in this book to credit my parents for putting up with me in my upbringing, I was a disaster for the best part of 20 years. For any of you reading this who are parents, maybe I can be an example of having confidence in your children; I honestly believe up until the age of 18 my parents would have taken me back to the adoption home if there was a returns policy. My biological father doesn't know I was ever born and my biological mother holds probably one of the highest positions of nobility within my life. I'll never meet the person I'm most grateful for. In 2021, adoption levels hit their lowest ever in the UK to 2,870, that's 0.042 per cent of the UK population. (See References, p. 263) I have a letter that's as old as I am; this letter in question was typed out on a typewriter, I keep it at home. It explains why I was adopted and the letter tells me about my Irish biological family. It says in the final chapter that *'she wanted a secure home for her son where all the opportunities to grow into a secure and happy young man would be available for him.'* I think that, when I think about it, one of the core drives I have within myself to do well, is to ensure that a brave decision that was made by a single woman in 1989 didn't go to waste. Reflecting as an older adult, I think that's one of my core reasons to get up and attack every day in front of me with everything I have. Our past shapes who we are, but we are not governed by it, we still have a choice how we perceive things and how we let them, yes, let them impact us each day. When I first publicly told people the fact I was adopted, I was pointed to literature to help understand some of the emotions adopted people can feel; however I didn't resonate with any of it. I see my past as a reason to be stronger, not to feel weaker. The same way I've learned over the years to use uncomfortable situations to challenge myself rather than shy away from my ambitions. I wasn't confident in my younger years, but it came as a decision that I had to make in school to make friends and as a necessity, then again in my professional life to become the person I needed in my life 10 years ago.

For yourself, I want you to really understand that whatever has happened before can be hugely advantageous. If you're someone of little confidence, you have so much room to grow. If you're someone fairly confident in most situations, but not all, you have a foundation in which to grow on. I'll say it again, do not dwell on what has happened to you, but instead appreciate it for what it is and use it to your advantage.

The Present

This is if anything the most important tense. It's a clear understanding of where you are now and what you're thinking right now. Our thoughts and how we handle and deal with them is make or break for the two sides of the coin that govern confidence; those two sides are action and inaction. When understanding the right tools to have in the present moment, nothing is better than understanding what is true and what isn't. One of the core principles behind breaking down limiting beliefs is to determine whether our thoughts are true. For instance, when I had to increase my prices as a personal trainer, my mind would be flooded with doubt and I'd create a hypothesis that I couldn't charge that higher amount, I'd believe it was true until I properly challenged it. This is why I believe there is so much misinformation rife in the world at the moment: we have the hypothesis and evidence dilemma that we assume things are true until proved otherwise, when instead we should be doing the complete opposite. People will use a rubbish supplement and ask for proof that it doesn't work. It should not have been for sale until its efficacy was proved in the first place. When scientists for years have had a hypothesis, it must remain a hypothesis until evidence proves it. Then even that often isn't enough and you'd look at meta-analyses of compared studies together to build only a stronger conclusion. If we were to pick any of your doubts, any of your limiting beliefs or any limitations you have on your potential or ability, I can guarantee you have deemed many of them true without any hard evidence to prove the hypothesis.

I always thought to myself, 'Could this hold up in court?' Imagine a jury. 'James Smith doesn't think enough people would pay him £40 an hour for personal training'. Ok sir, any evidence to prove this? Not really, just my negative thoughts, negativity bias and a few other hypotheses I have in my mind that I've curated off previous experiences. Imagine your own mini trial in your mind. 'I don't think it's possible to get a promotion (or pay rise) if I ask my boss'. Ok, do you have any real tangible evidence to support that idea? If not, then you cannot hold it as true in your mind. We must at any given opportunity fight our thoughts and put them to trial. Is this true? Could it hold up in court? If not, you must regard it as untrue until proven. I believe one of the main reasons humans lie is to keep each other safe, I believe it's why we create lies inside our own head. It's an automatic response to stop you taking risks; for the large part I bet the mechanism has saved thousands if not millions of lives over millennia time and time again. Parents lie to children to keep them safe too. 'Swallowing chewing gum takes seven years to digest'. This isn't true, but probably each year saves a few kids choking on their gum. 'Don't swim after eating, or you'll get cramps.' I think this is so that the parents don't have to be on lifeguard duty while they're still eating. Or that 'peeing in the pool will show up bright green.' That's not perhaps a life-saving lie, but one I'm grateful of nevertheless as someone who can swim with his mouth open. From reading this chapter, I really want you to challenge your thoughts and really probe them for truthfulness; by breaking down thoughts as untrue, you develop cases in your mind for being able to do things, not shy away from them. This in turn elevates your confidence by suppressing your doubts and insecurities.

Fuck luck. Yeah, that's right. I want you to eradicate your existing beliefs surrounding people being lucky. So much of luck is not luck, it's making good decisions. Don't ever for a second think someone got lucky getting a job, someone got lucky finding a great life partner, don't think for a second someone got lucky getting a pay rise or promotion. Luck does exist but not as much as we think it does. Even a good upbringing is a direct result of good decisions made before someone's birth. People make long-term good decisions that often play out well over time. So, when you look at your life now and where you would like it to be, don't wish for good luck, wish to make better decisions when they arise and when they present themselves to you. There are going to be moments that come up today, tomorrow, next week and beyond where you're faced with two paths, action versus inaction. If you wish to be lucky, you need to take action. You can't expect things to work out for you unless you work on acting in your best interest, to make the right decision when it arises.

The Unknown

Well, this is it, this is where I can't do any more for you. I have my own journey, my own life and my own experiences that I've drawn upon to reach this stage in the book. I've collated data and insights from those much smarter than me and done my best to present it to you. I've shared secrets, processes and insights to do one thing, to change the course of your life for the better. Now I don't expect you to wake up tomorrow a different person, but even just the slightest changes in perception on areas of your life will have a massive impact on where you end up in weeks, months and years ahead. I spoke before about so many people who get the knowledge they need to change their life and who let it fall on deaf ears. You are the director of this story, you get to decide how the next scene plays out and how each remaining chapter goes. Will it be easy? No. Will it be fun, not always. Will it work out? Not all the time. Will it be worth it? Yes. Fuck yes.

People tend to underestimate the amount of change that can happen from this moment on. I'm not saying you're going to end up being famous or a movie star, I'm not saying you're going to have a tech start-up that makes you millions. But what I do hope is that you end up becoming proud of your growth, however small or large it may be from today onwards. I hope that you have little moments where you're proud to be you, where you're so glad that you ended up existing in your own life. I hope to have instilled some level of tenacity and audaciousness into your passions, irrespective of what they are, and I hope that you have a new insight into your potential. I hope that when you put down this book you set your sights on your next goal and do everything in your power to obtain it. Life is great, it's shorter than we realise, we have primitive brains in modern societies, it's normal to lack confidence, it's normal to be scared, it's normal to be worried and it's normal to think of the worst outcome.

Not many, but some, not all, but enough people I believe have cracked the code of confidence and they've enriched their lives off the back of it, and that's all I want for you. I'm not going to pretend I know the depths of the meaning of life or why we're here, that's another book altogether. I do however have one request for you, one before I leave this book, one last thing I need from you. For all we know this could be the last thing I ever manage to write in a published book. I've done a rough calculation of what percentage our lifespan is of the universe thus far since its creation. It works out to 0.000000000054 per cent, so my last request is this: do everything in your power to please, make the most of it, confidently.

Thank you
James

References

p. 6 https://www.ncbi.nlm.nih.gov/pmc/articles/PMC5641835/

p. 23 https://www.cnbc.com/2021/11/09/ousted-wework-ceo-adam-neumann-47-billion-valuation-went-to-his-head.html#:~:text=Adam%20Neumann%2C%20CEO%20of%20WeWork.&text=Ousted%20WeWork%20CEO%20Adam%20Neumann%20said%20Tuesday%20that%20the%20company's,2019%20amid%20its%20botched%20IPO

p. 28 https://www.theatlantic.com/health/archive/2012/10/study-people-living-in-poverty-are-twice-as-likely-to-be-depressed/264320

p. 30 https://www.ncbi.nlm.nih.gov/pmc/articles/PMC8121294/#:~:text=For%20example%2C%20the%20joint%20life,both%20spouses%20have%20college%20degrees

p. 37 https://www.pewresearch.org/politics/2015/09/03/the-whys-and-hows-of-generations-research/

p. 38 https://www.pewresearch.org/fact-tank/2019/01/17/where-millennials-end-and-generation-z-begins/

p. 38 https://www.theguardian.com/world/2021/jun/02/a-sacrificed-generation-psychological-scars-of-covid-on-young-may-have-lasting-impact

p. 43 https://tim.blog/2007/12/10/how-to-get-george-bush-or-the-ceo-of-google-on-the-phone/

p. 44 Ferriss, T. *The 4-Hour Work Week* (Vermillion UK, 2011)

p. 45 https://pubmed.ncbi.nlm.nih.gov/17425538/

p. 46 https://www.oprahdaily.com/life/a30244004/how-to-manifest-anything/

p. 46 https://www.bmj.com/content/348/bmj.g3253

p. 51 Wray, N. and Visscher, P. (2008). 'Estimating trait heritability.' *Nature Education* 1(1):29

p. 53 https://en.wikipedia.org/wiki/Muggsy_Bogues

p. 56 https://www.bidmc.org/about-bidmc/news/2022/01/placebo-effect-contributes-to-covid-19-vaccine-adverse-events

p. 56 https://www.sciencedaily.com/releases/2012/12/121218121259.htm#:~:text=Summary%3A,to%20a%20major%20new%20study.&text=FULL%20STORY-,Half%20of%20the%20benefit%20of%20taking%20sleeping%20pills%20comes%20from,in%20the%20British%20Medical%20Journal

p. 59 https://www.mayoclinic.org/diseases-conditions/restless-legs-syndrome/symptoms-causes/syc-20377168#:~:text=Restless%20legs%20syndrome%20(RLS)%20is,eases%20the%20unpleasant%20feeling%20temporarily

p. 63 https://historyofyesterday.com/pavlovs-dog-the-experiment-that-revolutionized-psychology-d4bfdc343c73

p. 65 https://www.sciencedaily.com/releases/2018/09/180919115827.htm

p. 65 https://www.ncbi.nlm.nih.gov/pmc/articles/PMC3419487/

p. 66 https://www.ncbi.nlm.nih.gov/pmc/articles/PMC4552811/

p. 67 https://cdn.ymaws.com/www.psichi.org/resource/resmgr/journal_2013/Summer13JNCusack.pdf

p. 68 https://www.statista.com/statistics/645919/australia-number-of-ceos-by-gender/

p. 70 https://medlineplus.gov/genetics/understanding/inheritance/heritability/

p. 70 https://journals.sagepub.com/doi/abs/10.1111/j.1467-9280.1997.tb00458.x

p. 71 https://www.ncbi.nlm.nih.gov/pmc/articles/PMC1392256/

p. 71 https://www.cdc.gov/genomics/disease/epigenetics.htm

p. 71 https://www.ncbi.nlm.nih.gov/pmc/articles/PMC2084483/

p. 75 Vaish, A., Grossmann, T., and Woodward, A. (2008). 'Not all emotions are created equal: the negativity bias in social-emotional development.' *Psychological Bulletin 134* (3):383–403

p. 81 https://onlinelibrary.wiley.com/doi/abs/10.1111/j.1467-6494.1982.tb00745.x

p. 87 https://doi.apa.org/doiLanding?doi=10.1037%2F0022-3514.77.6.1121

p. 90 https://www.mcgill.ca/oss/article/critical-thinking/dunning-kruger-effect-probably-not-real

p. 92 https://www.businessinsider.com/the-most-dangerous-jobs-in-america-2018-7?r=AU&IR=T#3-roofers-32

p. 92 https://www.adelaidenow.com.au/business/sa-business-journal/nuclear-power-kills-fewer-people-than-solar-per-unit-of-electricity-says-university-college-london-professor-tim-stone/news-story/719096bad937b90f55dcc5c9f2ecc3fb

p. 93 https://www.simplypsychology.org/availability-heuristic.html

p. 94 https://ur.umich.edu/0203/Jan20_03/18.shtml

p. 94 https://www.floridamuseum.ufl.edu/shark-attacks/odds/compare-risk/death/

p. 94 https://pubmed.ncbi.nlm.nih.gov/30138002/

p. 95 https://www.rollingstone.com/feature/heavens-gate-20-years-later-10-things-you-didnt-know-114563/

p. 97 https://www.ncbi.nlm.nih.gov/pmc/articles/PMC3835346/

p. 98 https://papers.ssrn.com/sol3/papers.cfm?abstract_id=1800168

p. 98 Location of the hits in the aircraft. McGeddon, CC BY-SA 4.0, via Wikimedia Commons

p. 99 https://www.cantorsparadise.com/survivorship-bias-and-the-mathematician-who-helped-win-wwii-356b174defa6

p. 101 https://www.news5cleveland.com/before-you-go-gambling-the-best-and-worst-casino-game-odds#:~:text=1.-,Blackjack,to%20play%2C%22%20Bean%20said

p. 103 Rayner, G. and Brown, O. (2 May 2016). 'Leicester City win Premier League and cost bookies biggest ever payout.' *Telegraph*. ISSN 0307-1235. Archived from the original on 3 May 2016. Retrieved 5 August 2018

p. 106 https://asana.com/resources/social-loafing

p. 106 Simms, A. and Nichols, T. (2014). 'Social loafing: A review of the literature.' *Journal of Management Policy and Practice* 15(1):58–67. FROM –> https://www.verywellmind.com/what-is-social-loafing-2795883#citation-3

p. 110 https://slate.com/technology/2012/10/evolution-of-anxiety-humans-were-prey-for-predators-such-as-hyenas-snakes-sharks-kangaroos.html

p. 111 https://www.theatlantic.com/entertainment/archive/2010/04/there-are-always-more-of-them-before-they-are-counted/38998/

p. 114 https://www.hcamag.com/au/specialisation/financial-wellness/what-issues-are-impacting-employee-satisfaction/173994

p. 120 https://www.latimes.com/archives/la-xpm-2008-jan-13-op-schermer13-story.html

p. 126 https://www.ncbi.nlm.nih.gov/pmc/articles/PMC3809096/

p. 126 https://www.ncbi.nlm.nih.gov/pmc/articles/PMC4698595/

p. 127 https://www.cdc.gov/cancer/lung/basic_info/risk_factors.htm#:~:text=Cigarette%20smoking%20is%20the%20number,of%20more%20than%207%2C000%20chemicals

p. 128 https://www.16Personalities.com

p. 136 https://en.wikipedia.org/wiki/Intonation_(linguistics)

p. 137 https://psycnet.apa.org/doiLanding?doi=10.1037%2F1528-3542.7.3.487

p. 138 https://blog.ted.com/body-language-survey-points-to-5-nonverbal-features-that-make-ted-talks-take-off/

p. 138 https://www.emerald.com/insight/content/doi/10.1108/LODJ-07-2013-0107/full/html

p. 139 https://www.theidioms.com/fake-it-till-you-make-it/

p. 139 https://ideas.ted.com/inside-the-debate-about-power-posing-a-q-a-with-amy-cuddy/

p. 139 https://www.ted.com/participate/organize-a-local-tedx-event/tedx-organizer-guide/speakers-program/what-is-a-tedx-talk

p. 140 http://www.word-detective.com/2011/10/pinch-of-salt/#:~:text=So%20the%20truth%20is%20almost,bit%20of%20salt%20on%20it.&text=So%20the%20modern%20usage%20comes%20from%20bad%20medieval%20food

p. 141 https://pubmed.ncbi.nlm.nih.gov/15288702/

p. 141 https://psycnet.apa.org/buy/2015-04973-001

p. 143 https://psycnet.apa.org/buy/2015-04973-001

p. 149 https://www.podcastinsights.com/podcast-statistics/#:~:text=Also%2C%20a%20common%20question%20is,episodes%20as%20of%20April%202021

p. 150 https://harpersbazaar.com.au/tall-poppy-syndrome-wellbeing-mental-health/

p. 154 Breines, J. (April 2012). 'Call me crazy: The subtle power of gaslighting.' *Berkeley Science Review*

p. 155 https://www.researchgate.net/profile/Grant-Harris-4/publication/256486791_Credibility_of_repeated_statements_Memory_for_trivia/links/0deec5230e01875774000000/Credibility-of-repeated-statements-Memory-for-trivia.pdf

p. 157 https://www.science.org/content/article/identifying-brains-own-facial-recognition-system#:~:text=The%20ability%20to%20recognize%20faces,when%20people%20look%20at%20faces

p. 157 https://www.newtimes.co.rw/opinions/mere-mortals-obligation-serve#:~:text=Every%20time%20a%20citizen%20bowed,'re%20just%20a%20man.%E2%80%9D

p. 159 https://www.pnas.org/doi/10.1073/pnas.2100430118

p. 160 https://thedecisionlab.com/biases/pessimism-bias

p. 175 https://dontdisappoint.me.uk/resources/lifestyle/dating-statistics-uk/

p. 182 https://academy.sportlyzer.com/wiki/arousal-and-performance/inverted-u-hypothesis/

p. 186 https://www.ncbi.nlm.nih.gov/pmc/articles/PMC5351796/

p. 189 https://pubmed.ncbi.nlm.nih.gov/1484793/

p. 192 https://www.archimedes-lab.org/memorizing_numbers.html#

REFERENCES

p. 192 https://economictimes.indiatimes.com/magazines/panache/your-goldfishs-memory-lasts-longer-than-3-seconds-amp-other-facts-about-the-popular-pet/not-just-three-seconds/slideshow/65604290.cms

p. 203 https://psycnet.apa.org/record/2000-13328-002

p. 206 https://thedecisionlab.com/biases/declinism

p. 207 https://scholarworks.iupui.edu/bitstream/handle/1805/14820/Fang-2017-Does-bad-news.pdf?sequence=1

p. 215 https://www.reviews.org/au/mobile/aussie-screentime-in-a-lifetime/#:~:text=on%20our%20phones.-,What%20we%20found,percent%20of%20our%20waking%20life3

p. 222 https://www.ncbi.nlm.nih.gov/pmc/articles/PMC5364176/

p. 223 https://pubmed.ncbi.nlm.nih.gov/21495519/

p. 224 https://www.frontiersin.org/articles/10.3389/fpsyt.2021.705559/full

p. 224 https://pubmed.ncbi.nlm.nih.gov/18787373/#:~:text=Collectively%2C%20the%20cortisol%20findings%20support,HPA%20axis%20stimulus%20(ACTH)

p. 225 https://www.ncbi.nlm.nih.gov/pmc/articles/PMC4912993/

p. 226 https://www.medicalnewstoday.com/articles/320839

p. 226 https://www.mdpi.com/1422-0067/22/1/338

p. 232 https://journals.sagepub.com/doi/abs/10.1177/0956797610364751

p. 244 https://www.bgateway.com/assets/market-reports/Fitness-Leisure.pdf

p. 244 https://www.statista.com/topics/3411/fitness-industry-in-the-united-kingdom-uk/#dossierKeyfigures

p. 250 https://papers.ssrn.com/sol3/papers.cfm?abstract_id=934320

p. 250 https://www.ncbi.nlm.nih.gov/pmc/articles/PMC5089055/

p. 256 https://www.communitycare.co.uk/2021/11/22/children-adopted-from-care-falls-to-lowest-in-21-years-government-figures-show/

Acknowledgements

Thanks to my family, friends, Academy members, book buyers, talk attendees. Without your support there would be no book in front of you right now and no acknowledgements to read.

Index

ALSO AVAILABLE BY THE INSPIRATIONAL #1 *SUNDAY TIMES* BESTSELLING AUTHOR

If you enjoyed the book and would like to see more of what
I can do to help you in the next stage of your journey,
feel free to head to the James Smith Academy:

**James Smith
Academy**

www.jamessmithacademy.com

@Jamessmithpt